FIGHTING THE COLOR MONSTER

My Struggle to Overcome Racism

Written by

Harold K. "Hal" Brown

MONTEZUMA
PUBLISHING

San Diego, California

Published by
Montezuma Publishing
Aztec Shops Ltd.
San Diego State University
San Diego, California 92182-1701

619-594-7552

www.montezumapublishing.com

ISBN: 978-0-7442-7874-3

Publishing Manager: Kim Mazyck
Cover Design: Lia Dearborn and Angelica Lopez
Design and Layout: Lia Dearborn
Formatting: Lia Dearborn and Angelica Lopez
Quality Control: Joshua Segui

ABOUT THE AUTHOR

Harold K. "Hal" Brown was born in York, Pennsylvania in 1934. He made his way west to San Diego State College (Now San Diego State University) on an athletic scholarship after spending one semester at Penn State University. His career includes being an educator, civil rights leader, banker, U.S. Peace Corps administrator, civic leader and business man. He has a long history as a volunteer civil rights and community activist. Mr. Brown led San Diego's Congress of Racial Equality (CORE) in many protest demonstrations which resulted in several arrests and his spending many days in jail. In addition to the CORE activities, his volunteer work as a community activist also included the founding and directing of a number of community organizations.

Mr. Brown has received numerous honors and awards recognizing his achievements which include being selected by the U.S. Small Business Administration as the Minority Small Business Advocate of the Year for the United States; received the Boys and Girls Clubs of San Diego's highest achievement award; Named to the San Diego Business Journal's list of top 100 business and community leaders; served as President of San Diego's Holiday Bowl; and received the Human Dignity Award from the Jackie Robinson YMCA; the Drum Major for Justice Award from the Neighbor House Association; and the President's Award from the San Diego NAACP.

San Diego State University honored Mr. Brown by dedicating a campus tree which included a bronze plaque with his name placed at the base of the tree for his service to the university, its students, and the community. The San Diego State University Library developed a civil rights collection which include Mr. Brown's civil rights papers and named it the Harold K Brown Civil Rights and African American Experience Collection in honor of Mr. Brown. Mr. Brown was selected by San Diego State University as the recipient of its "Distinguished Alumni Award." He was also selected by the California Black Legislators as an "Unsung Hero of the Civil Rights Movement" and was honored on the floor of both the California State Senate and Assembly.

Mr. Brown received his undergraduate degree from San Diego State University and his Master's Degree in Business Administration from Fordham University in New York. In addition, he has completed courses toward a Ph.D. Degree in Business Executive Management at the Claremont Graduate School of Business Administration in

Claremont, California. Mr. Brown received an honorary doctorate degree, the Doctor of Humane Letters (L.H.D.) from San Diego State University.

Mr. Brown retired as the Associate Dean in the College of Business Administration at San Diego State University and currently serves as the President of BTW Development, Inc., a real estate and land development company.

CONTENTS

ACKNOWLEDGEMENTS

It takes a lot to get from where you started in life to where you are today. Being wherever I am today took a lot of help from a lot of people. It all started with my mother. She, in her quiet way, with her undying love and strong protection, provided me with the security that I needed to survive, whatever the obstacles might be. Her love and caring extended equally to all seven of her children and that love and caring were passed on to me, the baby of the family. Thank you Emma Brown for all you did to cause me to feel that I never wanted to disappoint you and to feel that whatever I did in life was to make you proud.

The words "It takes a village to raise a child" certainly apply to my life. In addition to my mother and family, many people have reached out to help that kid who needed help from those who were in positions to be helpful to a kid like me with no father in the home, a mother who had no education beyond the eighth grade, and who lived in a community where those conditions were ordinary.

Let me acknowledge some of those people, starting with my seventh grade home room teacher, Mrs. Cassandra Schade. She, a white teacher, was the first person to reach out to me, a colored boy in a predominantly white school, and made me feel welcomed and liked. She brought me into her extended family and made me aware of college and my scholastic ability to attend college. She, her husband and sons remained a part of my life and her example of caring has guided me throughout my life and inspired me to reach out to help others.

When I entered high school I was fortunate to have received close attention and caring from Mr. Vernon Ness, my home room teacher; Mr. Ed Walters, the faculty advisor for our debating society; and Mr. Waleski, my baseball coach. These teachers' influence in my junior high and senior high schools had and still have a dramatic effect on my life. It is important to note that there were no black teachers at those schools, so the caring I received came from teaches who were white, and I thank them for the influence they have had on my life. They are an important reason for my writing this book.

I was given an office in the San Diego State University Library which I used while writing this book. I can't thank the Dean of the Library, Dr. Gale Etschmaier enough for all the encouragement and support she has given me during this endeavor.

As I began writing this book, I contracted with Laura Close, BOSS News Network Publication, to be my editor. Laura used her experience and expertise to guide me through this long undertaking. Thank you Laura for your expertise, patience, and caring about the issues contained in this book.

I suppose ignorance and naiveté can be helpful to possess in one's life. If I knew how difficult and time consuming it would be to write this book, I don't believe I would have undertaken it, even knowing how desperately I feel about the importance of the book's message.

It seems that whatever I take on in life, there is always an angel beside me, helping to achieve my goal. How lucky I am to have that angel as my wife. During the entire writing of this book, my wife LaVerne has assisted me every step of the way. Every chapter that I completed writing, I asked her to review it and to give her comments, which she did. She also provided me with information that I was unable to recall. After all the chapters had been completed, I edited each chapter again, rewrote some things, and LaVerne re-read the chapters and provided me with wonderful editing and typing assistance. I chose to read all the chapters a third time and my wife again read and typed each chapter with the changes and additions I made. She then offered many helpful suggestions. In addition, LaVerne maintained all the chapters on the computer and updated the chapters with my changes and additions. I don't have the words to adequately express to my wife how grateful and appreciative I am for all her help in the writing of this book.

Finally, I thank Kim Mazyck, Associate Director, Montezuma Publishing, San Diego State University, the publisher of my book, and Lia Dearborn, Publishing Manager, for their assistance in getting the book out to the public. Their guidance and assistance have been very helpful and are very much appreciated.

My Mother, Emma C. Brown

INTRODUCTION

I have been haunted all of my life by race and the color of my skin. It has shaped me into who I am today, and influenced my life as much as education, religion, or health, or love, and I can't help but imagine how my life would have been without the influence of racism and color, and its control over the minds of Americans.

On three separate occasions I found myself standing in front of a judge, being sentenced to spend time in jail for objecting to the unjust treatment of African Americans in San Diego, California. Often I wondered "How did it get to this? And why me?"

This book is an attempt to explain how conditions dictated by race in America can cause a quiet, intelligent, fun-loving kid to land in jail filled with anger and disappointment. It shows what can happen to a kid's mind—and how closed off from others a person can become—when the color of his or her skin is considered more important than his or her abilities.

This book speaks to America, pleading for it to face head-on and remove the conditions caused by institutionalizing color as the means of controlling people to appear inferior to whites.

This book is a warning to America to be careful about how it treats its citizens, and to pay attention to the costs that are likely to result from the mistreatment of its people.

But this book also shows what it takes for a kid like me to grow into a valuable citizen. I am, today, viewed as a success. But, as my time in front of a judge implies, there was often a steep cost on the way to that success.

Why did I choose to write this book? Approximately twenty-five years ago it was suggested by a friend, Morris Casuto, who was the western director of the Anti Defamation League in San Diego, that I needed to write a book about the civil rights movement in San Diego. He went on to say that since I led the civil rights movement, who could better tell the story, and people need to know that part of San Diego's history. It took me twenty-five years to convince myself to do it. What helped to convince me was whenever I mentioned the civil rights movement in San Diego people were shocked that there was a civil rights movement in San Diego.

Another thing that convinced me to write this book is that I, the leader of that movement, owe it to the members and supporters of the Congress of Racial Equality (CORE) who fought heroically beside me to bring about the changes we enjoy in San Diego today.

This book is the story of one life—my life—which has to be a similar story of other African American men who were born in the 1930s and before. The book starts with my life at birth and reveals some of the incidents of how the color of my skin influenced my life and continues to do so even today.

The book is written to show the reader the potential destruction that this "color for power" game can cause. Some victims of the "color for power" game may have been able to overcome its effects, but many have not. It is my hope that this book will cause the reader to think deeply about this color issue and to take steps to join with others to eliminate the color monster.

CLARIFICATION

Since the arrival of slaves in America, the terms "colored" and "negro" have been used to describe them. As the decades have passed, this group of Americans chose to use "black" and "African American" as identifying terms, a trend which continues to this day.

During the near-century covered in this book from 1934-2018, the author uses the words popular at the time when discussing a particular period in his own history, and the country's history.

CHAPTER ONE

Early Life, Early Exposure

When I was six years old, my mother sent me off to the first grade in a school that was about a three and a half mile walk from our house. We passed by a white school to get to our colored school, which was about one and a half miles from my house. The walk in the rain and snow was not very pleasant. There was a chain factory on the way to the school, and as my friends and I passed it, I heard people yelling from the building. When I looked up, I saw some men sticking their heads out of the factory windows on the upper floors. They were shouting at us: "Nigger! Nigger! Nigger!"

That's when it first hit me. That's when I received the first notion that the color of my skin and the color of my friends who were walking with me, must be a problem for those men: "nigger" was the word they used to express that they did not like us. This was the first time I recognized that the color of my skin was a problem to others who were not my color. As I grew older, this color thing popped up time and time again, and I soon learned that the color of my skin would play a dominant role in my life and would hang over my head like a monster, waiting to strike at any time.

I arrived into this world May 6th, 1934 in the small town of York, Pennsylvania. The hospital would have been nice: clean, and the people would have seemed pleasant enough. But my mother knew something then that it would take me just a few short years to figure out.

The people around me at the hospital were different. They spoke the same language I would come to learn, they dressed about the same, but something was different. Their color was different from my mom's and mine.

After a couple days, my mom took me home. The next few days would have been filled with people in our home. Those who visited us to see my mom and me, our neighbors and friends, all had the same color as me and my mom. I remember the first four years of my life being littered with small revelations of the differences between these colors.

When I turned five, my mom moved us to another neighborhood closer to the center of town. That neighborhood was much like the other one: three blocks of old attached row houses in an alley.

In this neighborhood, two houses had people in them who, again, looked different from me. They looked like the ones I would have seen when I first came into this world. I also couldn't help but notice that all the houses surrounding our neighborhood had people living in them who didn't look like me, my mom, my sisters and brothers, and the others who live in the two neighborhoods I lived in so far.

This pricked my young curious mind but didn't really faze me. I was too busy having fun playing ball with the other children in the neighborhood.

So what hit me that first day of first grade? I realized, once again, that those men looked just like the people who helped deliver me into this world. They also looked the same as those who lived in the houses on the street surrounding the neighborhoods where I lived.

They had the same skin color, a different one from me. Then the epiphany came: there was something going on with this color thing.

What is it? I wondered. As I grew older I realized more and more what the difference in these two colors meant. It meant people who didn't even know you hated you and called you names that you learned were bad. It meant going to schools where all the students looked like you. It meant people who look like me lived in the alleys and backstreets: poor and "bad" neighborhoods.

It made me think of the neighborhoods I passed on the way to school. Those houses were on streets— not in alleys—and had red bricks, grass lawns, and trees. That was a lot different from where my friends and I lived with our families.

As I got a little older, I realized that there were people of the other color who also lived in those poor neighborhoods, although most of them did not. However, even in the alleys where I lived, the two colors did not mix. They didn't even talk to each other; during my elementary school years, we went to our separate school and they went to theirs.

It wasn't until I was in sixth grade that I had any contact with white kids from another school. I wouldn't be surprised if this was their first contact with kids of my color too. When I was a child, I noticed the division by color and what it meant to be my color. But that was the way things were, and it didn't seem to be a big issue with anyone, at least on the surface. So I continued to play ball with my friends and looked forward to going to junior high school.

Junior high school came with my teen years and more issues of color. I was now 12 years old, looking forward to playing basketball, football, and baseball with my friends. But I received a shock that I was not prepared for when I got to school.

Practically everybody at my new school was white: the same color as the people who delivered me in the hospital, the same color as those men in the chain factory who called us niggers, and the same as those who lived in the nice houses I passed on the way to school.

Wait a minute, I thought. *What am I doing here? Is this some sort of punishment?* I remember sinking down in the chair at my desk and staying quiet. Turns out, nobody told me that this was racial integration. In my mind, it was discomfort. At the time, I didn't realize how my earlier years affected my thinking, leaving me to feel uneasy around those who did not look like me, my family, and my friends. I didn't realize that seeing the nice homes and clean streets when we had the opposite, or that observing all the important jobs were held by people of a different color from me, would hit me like it did.

That first day of junior high, I found myself right in the middle and surrounded by all of "them."

Things were made a little easier when I realized that my homeroom and math teacher, Mrs. Cassandra Schade, seemed to like me. She befriended me and counseled me to think about going to college, a word I had not heard before. She told me how she worked as a house cleaner to pay her way through college. Mrs. Schade and her husband Tom, a school principal, were white and two of the most loving and caring people I met while attending school. I remained close friends with them until their deaths.

This gave me a little comfort, but not nearly enough to offset the feeling I had developed from watching those who seem to have it all while we had so little.

Why were things like this? Who made them like this? Why did the people who looked like me seemed to be on the outside of the functioning of the town, and "they" seemed to be on the inside?

Despite this discomfort, I was determined to make the most of it all. I knew I was good at school work and sports, and junior high school slowly became fun. I made the school basketball and football teams, I became captain of both teams, and was having a good time. I was popular: a star athlete, and I enjoyed the attention I received from my teachers and schoolmates. I even became close friends with some of my schoolmates who were of the other color, and I made the school academic honor roll. But this color difference thing kept nagging at me and popping up when I least expected it.

For example, one of the girls in my seventh grade homeroom came over to me one day and said, "Hal, I told my dad about you and he doesn't like you." I don't remember what I said. I probably said nothing. I don't know if she knew why her dad didn't like me, but I knew. He didn't even know who I was. I'm sure my classmate told her dad that I was a good basketball player and that I was colored. The color monster took over from there.

I use the term "color monster" to describe the incidents when the color of one's skin becomes the dominant, and many times the only, factor determining the outcome of a decision regarding you. Color has been used throughout America to discredit or give favor to a person based on the color of that person's skin. If your color is black it can have a monstrous affect on you as decisions affecting your life are made in a context of racial bigotry and prejudice.

The color monster also had another trick up its sleeve. I first noticed that when school was out for the day, we all went home to our separate neighborhoods: they went one way and my friends and I went the other way. We wouldn't see each other again until the next day. After school my colored friends and I would go to the recreation center in our neighborhood—Crispus Attucks—for afterschool activities, and the white kids would go to their recreation center. The only difference was that anyone with my color was not allowed in their recreation center, but they were permitted to attend ours if they wanted to. They never did.

I also realized that those of my skin color were not allowed in the city's YMCA, skating rink, or swimming pool. We had to swim outside of town in a place that was called "Cow Shit Run" by the older boys in our neighborhood because that's where the cows swam, or grazed, or did whatever they did in the water.

At junior high age I was learning that racial integration didn't go very far in integrating the people of these two skin colors. I was—already, as a child—beginning to get tired of watching how their skin color had the nice neighborhoods, good jobs, nice recreation facilities, and our skin color had the opposite.

I was also tired of being a citizen, but not a "full" citizen—of being a student, but not a "full" student. There was always a line you must not cross. How did you know when you got to that line? You just knew. An example was when our junior high school had a day at the roller skating rink just for our school, I was encouraged to attend, so I did. I had never been to a roller skating rink, and it sounded like a fun thing to do. I don't know how I got to the rink. It was too far away to walk so someone must have driven me there, probably Mrs. Schade. I arrived at the rink, put on my skates, and began to skate around the rink, all the while feeling uneasy. I was the only "colored" person in the rink and there I was skating around the rink by myself, feeling alone, self conscious, and feeling that all eyes were on me.

It didn't occur to me that I would be the only "colored person" there when I said yes to going to the rink with my schoolmates. So there I was skating around and around, hoping I would not fall and watching the other boys and girls skating together holding hands, or boys with their arms around the girls' waists, skating to the rhythm of the music. I was feeling very uncomfortable knowing that if a colored boy was seen skating with a white girl, holding hands, or with his arm around her waist, the girl would have been socially ostracized and her parents would probably have read her the riot act and force her to change schools.

While all of this was spinning around in my head, I felt someone skate up behind me and tap me on the shoulder. I looked around. It was Mrs. Schade, my homeroom and math teacher. She grabbed my hand and began to skate with me. Now, I really hoped I wouldn't fall. We skated a number of times together around the rink. Mrs. Schade always treated me like my two sisters treated me: with love and care. She was always there for me, cheering me on.

The skating party ended and I was so relieved and happy to get home and be around my family and friends, and go to Crispus Attucks Center where I could be with "my" people and not feel like an outsider. There was not enough Mrs. Schades to make up for the conditions a "colored" kid had to endure.

Anger began to set in as I watched how the white skin color gave them all the privileges, and people with my skin color were treated as inferior, not as good or as smart as them, and called derogatory, humiliating names. It was the thought of seeing my mother, whom I loved dearly, going through life along with my brothers, sisters, nieces, nephews, cousins, uncles, and friends, living under these conditions and being treated as though we were not as good as those with white skin.

I never discussed my feelings with anyone because I was too shy. But I knew I was as good as any of them, maybe better than most.

When I was in the eighth grade I fulfilled an assignment in English class to write a composition on the subject of our choice. I wrote about how I felt and how it was wrong for the white students to be allowed in the teenage club, called TAC, and my friends and I were not allowed to attend. I never did get a response to the composition I wrote.

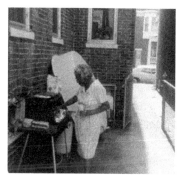

(left) Me, my mother, and brother, Lou (right)

My mother barbecuing

Me and my three oldest brothers,
Charles, Roy, and Paul

My nieces and nephews

My two sisters Geraldine and Evelyn

My nieces, nephews, cousins, and family

My nephews and their friend

My nephews and their friend

My sons, nieces, grand niece, and grand nephew

My close friend Jack, his wife, and their children

Another example of how the color of my skin affected my life during my junior high school years was when I attended music class and our music teacher, who was white, would on a regular basis choose the song "Old Black Joe" as one of the songs for the class to sing. Many years later my colored friends and I recalled the misery we experienced when singing that song in class. I remember hating to sing that song because of the use of the word "black" to describe Joe in the song. This was one of those sink-into-your-chair moments and we wished that the song would hurry up and end.

This is how I spent my early teenage years, developing anger about how "their" color lived and how "they" treated us. What kept my anger from exploding was my scholastic success; a few kind and supportive teachers like Mrs. Schade; a few white schoolmate friends; and my success as an athlete. Also, I was having fun playing sports and hanging out with my "colored" friends. I was growing up. Despite this anger, there was lots of fun and laughter in my family and I enjoyed being around my mom and brothers and sisters.

Playing with the other boys in our neighborhood was fun, but I had fun in our home as well. I was the last of seven born to Emma Charlotte Berry Brown. Being the baby of the family—with five boys and two girls—I am sure I enjoyed certain privileges. I felt very protected by a strong and caring mother who would give a hard spanking when you deserved it, while defending and supporting you with all of her might.

Since I grew up without a dad in the home, my mom was my rock. My brothers and sisters and my mom provided me with a great amount of security by supporting me with love and protection.

My three older brothers and my older sister were not living with us when I was growing up. I grew up with a sister and a brother in the home, and life in the home was filled with fun, laughter, music, and dancing. My mother did domestic work and found work where she could in order to feed and clothe us and to keep a roof over our heads. My mother and her brother, who shared the house with us, shared the housing expenses. Because of the love and great respect my brothers, sisters, and I had for our mother, that love also extended to each other.

I was a happy kid with lots of friends and family, which included an aunt, two uncles, nieces, and nephews and lots of cousins in the town where I lived. We all lived in our respective "colored" neighborhoods and everyone went about living their lives under racially segregated and racially discriminating conditions, but not a word was spoken about it. But this color monster hung over my head, and I carried it with me to high school.

My high school years were pretty much the same as my time in junior high. Most of my time was spent playing sports and trying to earn a scholarship to go to college. But racially, this color thing was still in full operation. My success in basketball and baseball grew stronger, and so did my anger for the way the people of my color were being treated in our town and our country.

I began reading *Jet Magazine*, a black-owned national magazine which reported racial incidents around the nation. While the magazine published the accomplishments of black people, it also reported about racial discrimination, lynchings, and how the National

Photo from Jet Magazine. One of many lynchings used as recreation for whites designed to terrorize Negroes

Association for the Advancement of Colored People (NAACP) and other groups were fighting to make it better for Negroes.

Again, I kept everything inside and never spoke to anyone about my feelings. My friends knew about the conditions we lived under as well as I did, but we didn't talk about it. Everyone, black and white, seemed to accept the racial condition for what it was—bad—and nothing could be done about it.

I considered my high school years to be very successful. I was taking college preparatory classes, was elected vice president of our senior class, and was even nominated to run for school president, but was convinced by a school counselor that I should not run for the position because of the amount of time being president would require, and playing sports would not allow me enough time to do both. I bought her story and declined the nomination, although I felt all along that she did not approve of having a Negro as president of the student body. I wish I had not taken her advice. Maybe she was correct, but having a student body president of my color would have been a first in the city of York and would have sent a message to our city that many probably would not have liked.

My high school career in sports was going very well. I was determined, at this point of my life, to accomplish four things: to earn a scholarship to go to college, to play college basketball and baseball, to play professional baseball, and to be a school teacher. I wanted to be successful. I wanted to make my mother proud and see the smile and pride on her face when she read in the newspaper or heard about how her baby "starred" in sports. I wanted to make my brothers and sisters proud of their brother. I wanted to show "white" people what we "colored" people could do—to prove to them that we colored people were as good as any other group of people and many of us were even better. My success in high school sports continued. I made the varsity starting team in basketball and baseball my first year. I became the captain in both sports. I won the basketball scoring title in our district by being the highest scorer and was named to the All State Pennsylvania First Team in basketball, following my brother, Lou, who was three grades ahead of me and the first from our high school to receive that honor. I was selected to be the starting shortstop to play at Yankee Stadium in New York

William Penn High School Year Book - 1952

in the game between the Eastern United States and the Western United States. I was also a member of the Alpha Debating Society and president of the Varsity Club. I was having fun in high school, mostly because of my success in sports. But, the color monster was still there.

Off the basketball court and baseball field, things were still the same as they were when I was born. People of my color were still forced to live in certain rundown areas of the city and were not permitted to join the YMCA, swim in the city's pool, or skate at the city's roller skating rink. People of my color could not eat in the restaurants or stay in the hotels. There were no teachers with my color teaching in any of the schools except in the two elementary schools for colored kids. There were no people of my color employed as police, firemen, lawyers, judges, one medical doctor, no dentists, no nurses, no business owners, etc.

In my senior year in high school this color monster jumped up and slapped me hard in the face. I had high hopes of becoming a professional baseball player and no one could tell me that I was not going to be the next Jackie Robinson, a baseball player who was the first Negro to play for a major league baseball team and was playing for the Brooklyn Dodgers. I loved me some Jackie Robinson! But my success as a baseball player was no match for the color monster.

One day at baseball practice, one of the scouts for the Philadelphia Phillies major league baseball team, who was at our practice to scout players on our team, came over to me and said he could not scout me because the Philadelphia Phillies were not signing Negro players, and he was sorry.

Me sliding at my high school baseball practice session

I was seriously hurt, crushed. *Don't tell me*, I thought, *that this color thing is going to keep me from fulfilling my dream to become a professional baseball player.*

Again, I shared my feelings with no one, and I told no one what the scout had said. I'm not exactly sure why I never told anyone about how I felt regarding what the scout had told me. In addition to being fairly quiet and shy, I knew there was nothing anyone I knew who would be able to do anything about it. Besides, I grew up in a family where you took what you had to take and not be a "cry baby." A boy was supposed to be tough, be a man, not a complainer. So, I knew what I had to do. I instead reminded myself that Jackie Robinson made it. He plays for the Brooklyn Dodgers, and I can make it too. I convinced myself I didn't want to play for the

Philadelphia Phillies anyhow. I wanted to be a Brooklyn Dodger like Jackie Robinson. So I fought back my tears, wiped away the scout's words, and continued to play well and keep my dream alive, hoping that things would change.

The last blow in high school came against me and the other "colored" students in my graduating class. Our senior year was coming to an end and we were all getting ready for our senior class picnic. We discovered that the venue where the picnic was going to be held, which was outside of York, did not allow Negroes to swim in their pool. This infuriated me and my friends so we decided not to attend our graduation picnic. These racial incidents were getting under my skin more and more: I was just 18 years old.

By the time I reached my senior year in high school I knew this racial thing pretty well. In spite of it all, I had some enjoyable times. One of the enjoyable times during my senior year was when I received the "Boy of the Month" award from one of the civic organizations in York. My mother and my oldest sister joined me at the event.

With all the awards and honors I received while growing up, no one in my family had ever been there when I received them. This time was different.

My baseball coach—Mr. Waleski, who was white—drove me speedily from the baseball game we were playing against a high school in another city. I had to change from my baseball uniform to street clothes while he was driving in order to get back to York in time for the event and the presentation.

When we arrived back in York I looked like a mess, but when I saw my mom and my sister seated at the event waiting for me to arrive, it became one of the happiest moments of my life. I had no idea they would be there.

I don't remember where the event was held, but most likely it was held at a hotel, and my mom and my sister must have felt very much out of place. During those years, colored people were not allowed in the hotels unless they were carrying the bags of hotel guests, setting up tables—which my brother, our friends, and I did—or you were one of the waiters. Even in good times, like being honored at an event, the color monster was there with its ugly presence.

Introspection

I grew up as a somewhat socially shy kid who was comfortable among family and close friends, but rather quiet and shy outside those circles, except for sports. That shyness remained with me for many years. I was not a kid who raised his hand in school to answer questions unless the teacher called on me. In junior high, I was on the honor roll and a popular athlete. In high school, in addition to being popular in sports, I was the president of the varsity club and vice president of our senior class. At the time, I was captain of our high school varsity basketball and baseball teams.

But even though I was in positions of leadership, I was not comfortable in social settings. I never sought the spotlight or brought attention to myself. Attention just came to me, mostly because of sports. My shyness and some social situations caused me to perspire heavily, which made me embarrassed, and caused me to perspire even more. The perspiring was not because of a lack of confidence: I had plenty of that.

I searched my mind for years as to why I was so uncomfortable in certain situations. I finally concluded that the discomfort I felt surfaced when I felt I did not have control in a particular situation and when I felt different and out of place from those around me. I felt very different around white people. My life was surrounded by the black-white comparison.

My brain was steeped in the propaganda of white is good, black is bad: white rich, black poor, white smart, black dumb, white clean, black dirty, white angel, black devil, white power, black no power, white teacher, white doctor, white lawyer, white mayor, white president.

White people went to big white churches, had golf courses and country clubs, and owned the hotels, department stores, and restaurants. All the years of growing up my brain was absorbing all this data, processing and storing it in a disk of inferiority and a disk of superiority. My brain from birth was trained to think and react to people in terms of the colors white and black.

To think in terms of white and black in our society can cause one to have any number of reactions: fear, hate, lack of motivation, intimidation, and over aggressiveness. My reaction came out in sports and social settings. I was determined not to let any white boy beat me in sports, and I perspired when in some social settings with white people. Since I was gifted with being very good in sports, my unrealistic determination to never let a white boy beat me in sports was largely upheld. My reaction of perspiring at social interactions with whites when I was not in control was most embarrassing.

Two such occasions stand out in my mind. One was when our high school debating fraternity was attending a program in the community. I was the only black person in the organization, and as we set in a group I began to perspire and could not stop no matter how hard I tried. I was ever so glad when the program was over.

The other occasion was when I was being interviewed by the local TV station. I had just been named to the all Pennsylvania State basketball first team and the TV station wanted to interview me in recognition of that honor. When the interview began I started to perspire. I took the handkerchief out of my pocket, which I brought with me just in case, and began to wipe the perspiration from my face. I continued to perspire throughout the interview. I was so embarrassed. The next day at school I was teased a little by my homeroom teacher for pulling out my handkerchief and wiping my brow. My homeroom teacher was my advisor and like a surrogate uncle, and was having fun teasing me. I smiled, but was still embarrassed. I was glad that none my family or friends had a TV set, or they would have teased me too.

CHAPTER TWO

College Days

As my mom, my sister, and I walked home from the awards ceremony, my mind was on college. I didn't have access to money to pay for college: all I had were sports trophies, newspaper headlines, and one scholarship offer. No one in my family had any money beyond what they earned at low-paying jobs to support their families. So, my only hope was to get a scholarship by playing sports.

Did I talk about my going to college with my family? No. I did not discuss it with them because I knew that they would be supportive but had no concept of what it would take for me to go to college and they had no way of assisting me financially.

I had been counseled by my homeroom teacher, Mr. Vernon Ness that I should attend Penn State University. He wanted me to play ball at some college in the state of Pennsylvania and he felt that I could receive financial assistance from the York Penn State Alumni Association. Mr. Ness was like a surrogate uncle to me. He watched over me and guided me and made sure that I made the right choices in school. He counseled me often to not just become a jock, which meant "play sports, but get a good education," So, I listened to his advice and applied to Penn State.

When I submitted my application to Penn State I was told by Mr. Ness that the Penn State Alumni Association would provide me with a scholarship. I was admitted to Penn State and, after being interviewed by the Penn State Alumni Association in York, I was awarded a scholarship. It paid for my tuition and books, but nothing was ever said about paying for my meals or a place to live. I was determined to go to college and play varsity basketball and baseball, and my immaturity and shyness did not allow me to ask questions, so I went along with going to Penn State.

Now, how was I going to get to Penn State and where was Penn State anyhow? I did not have a car, no one in my family had a car, or had access to one. Fortunately, some of the teachers at my high school were very supportive, encouraging and helpful to me. One of those teachers was my high school advisor, Mr. Ed Walters, who was the advisor for the Alpha Debating Society of which I was a member. He somehow knew that I did not have transportation to Penn State and that I did not have an overcoat for the bad winter weather. He bought me an overcoat for the cold weather and drove me to Penn State to begin my college career. He did this without my asking. He dropped me off at a house where I was to live, gave me a farewell handshake, and wished me well. I don't know who made the arrangements for me to live at the house, but Mr. Walters knew where to take me. The lady of the house showed me to my room. She told me that one other student would have a room there also. I met this student once and never saw him again.

I sat in my room. I was very lonely. I knew no one at Penn State or anyone who lived anywhere near Penn State. The only person I knew who was scheduled to attend Penn State was another athlete who was recruited by Penn State to play football. His name was Lenny Moore who played football for Penn State and later became a National Football League star. I knew Lenny from when we played sports at different high schools. I felt good that there was at least one person at Penn State that I knew.

The house where I was living was about a mile and a half from the campus. So, I walked to the campus to find something to eat and I tried to contact Lenny. I found Lenny, we visited and I met several others who were also athletes. We talked for several hours and I felt much better about being at Penn State.

I was now in college, but I did not count on having to make arrangements for paying rent and how I would get my meals. I made the assumption that meals would be a part of the scholarship. I had a place to live, but I only had the money that I had saved from working during the summer to use to pay for my meals, and that was not enough.

The cook at a fraternity house, Mrs. Edie Rollins, was also from York and a friend of my mother's. When she found out that I was attending Penn State, she told my mother to tell me to contact her and she would let me work at the university fraternity house washing pots and pans for my meals.

I worked at the fraternity house during the lunch hour and Miss Edie, as we called her in York, would sometimes pack some food for me to eat at dinner in my room. I also had a job on campus operating an addressograph machine, which was a machine that placed names and addresses on envelopes.

Now, the next problem was paying the rent for my room. I wrote to my high school teacher Mr. Walters, and explained that

I didn't have any money to pay my rent. He sent me the money. I now had my meals and rent for the month settled, and could now concentrate on my classes and basketball.

I was doing well in basketball, but not so well in my classes. My first year of college was not fun. I was working two part-time jobs. One job earned my lunch meals and the other helped to buy my dinners. I didn't even have money to pay rent or repair the soles on my shoes. I was attending basketball practice each day and playing games during some evenings. I was trying to manage these things while carrying a full academic class schedule. In addition, I did not know how to properly study for college courses.

I was frustrated and very lonely. I was also disappointed that I was at Penn State to play basketball on a scholarship and discovered that I had not received an "athletic" scholarship from the university. The money I received from the York Alumni Association was not for an "athletic" scholarship. If I had received an "athletic" scholarship I would have lived in a dormitory and would have been provided meals. I was very appreciative of the financial support from the York Alumni Association, but by not having an "athletic" scholarship meant that the university would not be providing my housing and meals. This made attending college for me very difficult and very unsettling.

As usual, throughout my life I did not share any of this with my mother and family. What could they have done? My family did not have the financial resources or the information necessary to advise me. I always felt that I should be able to solve my problems myself.

I found out that Omega Psi Phi, a black fraternity, had a vacant room in their fraternity house. I moved into that room where I had a roommate, and where there were other black students, which helped me to better adjust to being away from home.

While struggling with my classes, playing basketball, and having no money for things like haircuts, shoe repairs, and other incidentals, I received a letter at home from a scout for the St. Louis Browns major league baseball team inviting me to come to their minor-league spring training camp. I was very excited to receive that letter and felt that I now had an escape from Penn State.

But lurking behind every corner of course is the color monster, grinning and cackling, reminding you that it is always there. The envelope in which my letter was delivered contained the word "Colored" next to my name. I thought that was strange and my family and I laughed about it and found the humor in it, as we always seemed to do. At least the St. Louis Browns invited me for a tryout, which was more than I experienced with the Philadelphia Phillies, the Philadelphia Athletics, and the other major league teams.

I accepted the St. Louis Browns' invitation and left Penn State. When it was time to go to spring training in March 1953, I packed a little bag with my baseball spikes and glove and headed to spring training in Thomasville, Georgia. I boarded the train in York and made my way to Cincinnati, Ohio. I arrived in Cincinnati, and got in line for my next train the rest of the way there.

The conductor standing in front of the line was directing each passenger to walk to the right or to the left. As I entered the coach after the conductor directed me, I noticed that all the passengers in that coach were black. I also noticed that there didn't seem to be any windows in that coach. *Damn*, I remember thinking. *This is what I have been reading about in Jet Magazine.*

When I arrived in Thomasville, I received two surprises. The first was that all the other players were physically in shape and ready to play at full speed. I didn't know you had to be in shape when you got there—ready to run hard and throw hard. The scout hadn't given me that information. The second surprise was that color thing again. All the colored players were assigned to live in one of the barracks and all the white players were assigned to live in another barrack. For some reason, despite all of my other life experiences with this color thing, I hadn't expected that.

Although I knew about the conditions for Negroes in the South, and the conditions Negroes lived under in my hometown, I didn't expect it at a baseball training camp. I shouldn't have been surprised because of my experience in Cincinnati while traveling to spring training.

It was not my nature to accept abuse without a fight but I had my mind on one thing: becoming a professional baseball or basketball player. Eventually, I ruled out basketball because I didn't have enough height, so it had to be baseball. I was sure I was going to be another Jackie Robinson. Daily practice sessions began and I was doing well at my shortstop position, but the color monster's ugly head once again popped up.

One day at practice my legs were hurting so I left practice a little early and went to our trainer to have my legs treated. When my treatment was finished, I saw that our practice session had ended and the players had left the field. My glove and spikes were still at the field. The field was located near the woods, and was a long walking distance from the trainer's room and the barracks and it was beginning to get dark. As I walked down the wooded path toward the playing field, I saw several white men standing in a group next to a tree. My heart began to pound heavily. There was no one else around and my mind began racing. I was thinking "How am I going to get past this group of white men standing in the path where I was walking?" I was scared to death. I just knew I would be lucky to get by them and back to the barracks only by experiencing insults and name calling. As I got closer to the playing field, one of the men in the group yelled to me, "are you looking for these?" as he held my glove and spikes in the air. I guess I said yes. I was so scared, I don't know if I said anything. I walked over to them to get my glove and spikes and one of the men said to me, "We were watching these for you because those niggers over there steal," as he pointed somewhere a distance away. They handed my glove and spikes to me and I turned around and began walking back to the barracks. I was still scared and could not believe that my ears heard what I had just heard.

I could never figure out how this man could refer to the people he pointed toward as niggers who steal, and be talking to me, a black kid. Did my wearing a baseball uniform make me different in his eyes? Well, I was so glad to get back to the barrack safe and sound. I never thought about it again until much later. However, injuries at training camp from not being physically in shape resulted in my being sent home and not making the team.

I tried playing while injured but my throwing arm would not heal, and I pulled my groin muscle in both legs. This was the first time that I had not made a team that I tried out for, and I was crushed. Now I had to face my family and friends and tell them that I didn't make the team.

I was too hurt to get angry at the segregated conditions going back home, but I stewed in those exact conditions as I rode the segregated trains and sat in the segregated waiting room waiting for the next train. When I arrived home, I immediately contacted the basketball coach at San Diego State College (now San Diego State University) who had offered me a scholarship before I attended Penn State. I told him I would like to transfer to San Diego State. The coach said his offer for a scholarship was still there and he would expect me to arrive in San Diego in September.

I spent the summer in York working at a job I found and saved my money to go to San Diego State. When September rolled around, I was all packed and ready to go. I would be traveling to California with a friend from York, Ernest Hartzog, who was a student at San Diego State and also was a basketball player there and is now retired from Portland Public Schools as Assistant Superintendent.

On the day we were leaving, Ernie and two others who were also going to San Diego were in the car with him. As Ernie pulled up to our house to pick me up, my mother and other family members were all outside to see me off. As I climbed into the car I heard a voice calling my name coming from a window upstairs next door. It was my cousin, Ruthie, who threw something down to me. It was two dollars balled up. I had been holding back my tears up until then, I could no longer hold back my tears. That was one of the most tender moments of my life. Ruthie, like most of the colored people that I knew in York, was among the lower income group. Two dollars back then in 1953 was important to Ruthie. It meant that she was wishing me success and it was a token of encouragement and support. It also was meant to say good luck to me and "go get 'em." I have never forgotten that, and it has always served as an inspiration to me.

Our trip across country, a 3,000-mile trip, was one long big fight with the color monster. It was September 1953 and racism in the United States was strong. Segregated hotels and restaurants were commonplace throughout America. So, traveling from York, Pennsylvania to San Diego, California, without having a hotel where you could sleep, a bathroom you could use, or a place where you could eat made the trip miserable. I don't recall having packed any food. I recall stopping at gas stations and buying sandwiches and drinks to eat in the car. Ernie and I did the driving. The other two persons riding with us did not know how to drive a car.

In total over my college career, I made five trips by car from York to San Diego and San Diego back to York. Each trip was made under segregated conditions. On one trip there was one student who rode with us who was white. We would give him the money to go into restaurants along the way and buy the food that we would eat in the car.

After arriving in San Diego, Ernie and I went to his place where he lived in housing provided for San Diego State students who were military veterans. The next day I contacted San Diego

State's head basketball coach. I met with him and he informed me that according to NCAA rules, I would lose a year of eligibility if I enrolled at San Diego State and played basketball. That meant I would have to wait a year before I could enroll at San Diego State if I did not want to lose a year of eligibility to play basketball. The coach then told me that if I enrolled at San Diego Junior College, I could play basketball there for one year and I would not lose a year of eligibility at San Diego State.

I took the coach's advice and enrolled at San Diego Junior College, only to find out later that if I played basketball at the Junior College, I would lose a year of my eligibility to play at San Diego State. By this time I had enrolled at the Junior College and was taking a full load of classes, so, I decided to finish the year at the Junior College, not play basketball there, and wait until next year when I would enroll at San Diego State.

While attending the Junior College, I didn't know how I would keep my basketball skills sharp since I was not eligible to play at San Diego State at that time, and would lose another year of eligibility if I played at the Junior College. I was fortunate enough to be contacted by a person from Vista, California who informed me that he was putting together a team to represent Vista in a basketball tournament in Las Vegas. He asked me if I would be interested in being one of the players, of course I said yes. He also asked my two friends who were playing on the Junior College team to also join the team. Now, this was beginning to sound like fun and I was looking forward to playing in Las Vegas.

If there was one thing you could count on back then, is that the color monster would pop up its ugly head, show its ugly teeth, and snarl at you. When we arrived in Las Vegas my eyes were popping at seeing the lights, casinos, and all the excitement of people walking the streets. But that excitement soon turned into disgust when our coach could not get a hotel room for me and my two friends who were also black. To my surprise, Negroes were not allowed to stay in the hotels. After some trying, the coach was able to find a hotel room for us.

If that incident was not bad enough, this next one affected me even more. One day during the tournament, the coach decided to take us to one of the casinos, which one it was, I have no idea. When we entered the casinos, a man stopped us just as we walked inside the door and waved our coach to come to him. The coach then waved to us to turn around and leave the casino. Our coach said nothing to us, he didn't have to, my two friends and I knew why our team was turned away. We found out that Negroes were not allowed in the casinos. At that time I was nineteen years old, had grown up in a town with lots of segregation, where "colored" people could not rent a room in a hotel, but I was completely caught off guard and angered by these two experiences in Las Vegas. Somehow, under those circumstances, one of my friends and I were selected as "two of the outstanding five players of the tournament".

In later years I discovered that Joe Louis, who was then the heavyweight boxing champion of the world, who was one of my idols, and all the black entertainers who performed in Las Vegas, were not allow in the casinos other than to perform. This information did not make me feel any better – it made me feel worse.

Well, the school year ended and I, along with three friends who were from East Chicago, Indiana began our trip back east. They were also attending the Junior College and played basketball there. We were in my car which my brother had bought for me to return to college when I was at home for the previous Christmas holidays. My brother Charles, was a wonderful brother who would always find a way to help his younger brothers and sisters, and of course our mom. Charles worked on the trash trucks for the city of York, PA. He didn't have much, but he had enough to give my brother and me a couple of dollars after our basketball games to buy a hamburger and milkshake. Somehow he was able to buy a car for me to travel back and forth to San Diego to attend college.

While at home during the summer, I thought I had better check my military draft status to make sure that I would not receive a draft notice as soon as I returned to college. When I checked with the draft office, I was told that my name was close to being called for the draft. So instead of waiting, I volunteered to be drafted right away so I could complete my military obligation before returning to California. I was drafted into the U.S. Army in November, 1954. I spent two years in the Army where I played basketball and baseball at Fort Monmouth, New Jersey, in addition to my daily duties.

At this stage of my life I had become very familiar with the color monster and I knew it was lurking in every corner, especially in the South. During my basic training at Camp Gordon Georgia, a few friends and I went into town on a weekend pass. As we walked around town we saw signs on the doors of bars with the words "No Colored Allowed." We soon returned to our barracks. The other weekends that we had free were spent sometimes going to movies on the base, reading, and writing letters.

After basic training in cryptography, I was assigned to the Signal Corps at Fort Monmouth in New Jersey. While at Fort Monmouth, we were then ordered to participate in Army war games maneuvers in Louisiana. I said to myself, *no way am I going there.* Without thinking about going through the military chain of command, I went directly to the Base Commander and asked him why I should be sent to Louisiana where Negroes are treated so badly. He politely listened and then dismissed me. I never heard any more about it, which meant *get your gear packed, you're going to Louisiana.*

After several months in Louisiana we returned to Fort Monmouth in New Jersey. While at Fort Monmouth I took a big step and got married to my first wife, whom I met in high school. We were married in Newark, New Jersey. After serving the rest of my time at Fort Monmouth, I finished my time in the Army in November 1956 and went back to San Diego with my new wife and enrolled at San Diego State College.

My years as a student at San Diego State were pleasant. As a student athlete I had a number of good experiences and met some very nice people, both students and faculty. But that color thing, the color monster, was present there too. This color thing is all over this country, even out here in California, segregated fraternities and sororities, segregated housing, and employment discrimination in the city of San Diego. This is just like the town I grew up in. I thought, *am I going to have to live with this color thing hanging over my head all my life?*

Another color incident was when I was elected to the Student Council at San Diego State. As the Upper Division Representative, I was assigned the responsibility of chairing the Constitutions Committee. One of my duties was to review and recommend approval of the constitutions of all campus fraternities and sororities. When I received a copy of each constitution, I saw where some contained the wording that its membership was restricted to white males for the fraternities and white females for the sororities. I had no idea this wording was included in these constitutions, but there was no way that I was going to ignore that it was there. So, of course I did not recommend those that had that wording in their constitution for approval as an on campus organization. The issue never received much attention as I recall. I did not raise a ruckus over this issue as I would have in my later years, but I did my job. The issue was taken up by the two deans who were advisers to the Council but I don't know whether those who had that language included were permitted to have on-campus status. I went on with my life of playing basketball and pursuing my degree.

The only experience I had as a student at San Diego State where this color thing popped up again was when some of us who were members of the Wesley Foundation, a Methodist student organization on campus, formed a group to speak to church youth groups on the subject of race relations. I enjoyed doing this because it gave me an opportunity to address the problems confronting Negro citizens. At each church I spoke on the topic of self esteem and how the race issue could contribute to low self esteem among young children.

I continued playing basketball until my eligibility ran out at the completion of my first semester as a senior—I had used one semester of my eligibility while playing as a freshman at Penn State. During my senior year a very important event took place in my life: I became a proud father. Michael David Brown was born on February 22, 1959. I am very proud of Michael, who earned a PhD at the University of Maryland and is currently leading research teams in the study of hypertension among African Americans and is teaching Kinesiology as a professor at the University of Illinois at Chicago.

I completed my baccalaureate degree at San Diego State with a great sense of accomplishment. I earned a degree, fulfilled my dream of playing college basketball and baseball, became a member of Kappa Alpha Psi Fraternity, won a seat on the student council, was a member of the Blue Key Honor Society, and was named to Who's Who in American Colleges and Universities. I was now ready to start searching for a teaching position to fulfill my life's ambition.

With a fresh college diploma and teaching credential in hand, I decided to apply for a teaching position in the La Mesa Spring Valley School District just a few miles from downtown San Diego, CA. I was currently living temporarily in La Mesa, house sitting for a friend, Dave Neptune, who was in Arizona with his family working with a Native American Tribe. Dave was the director of the San Diego State University's YMCA. I worked my scholarship hours as David's assistant.

When the word got out in the La Mesa neighborhood that I would be moving into the Neptune's house, the color monster went into action. The Neptunes informed me that the people in the neighborhood were meeting at the church to protest my moving into "their" neighborhood. The Neptunes asked me if I still wanted to move in under those circumstances. I didn't grow up to be fearful, so I immediately said yes, even though I had a wife and a young son to protect. Somehow I didn't think the protesters had the courage to directly confront me.

When I shared my situation with some of my black friends, they wanted to spend the nights guarding the house in which we would be living, with weapons to protect us. I refused their offer because I was not afraid and I didn't feel that my family and I were facing any real danger, I was correct.

ON CAMPUS · SAN DIEGO STATE UNIVERSITY

Me, going to a meeting on San Diego State University campus.

We moved in and the only protests I experienced was from the building or extension of a high fence by the next door neighbor that separated the Neptune's house from the neighbor's house. The only other incident I experienced, as a result of my moving into the La Mesa neighborhood, was when the Neptunes returned, they had arranged for me to rent a house their friends owned a few blocks away. When we were moving into the house, a moving truck at the house across the street was moving that family out. (coincidence?). The other experience was the dumping of garbage on our lawn.

With this "welcome" to the neighborhood, I took out my college degree and teaching credential, gave them a kiss and drove to the La Mesa Spring Valley School District's office and informed the receptionist that I was there to apply for a teaching position. Then the color monster must have really gotten mad. When the receptionist escorted me to the office where I met with the person who casually told me that for me to teach in the La Mesa Spring Valley School District they would have to see if the people living in the school district would agree to having a Negro teaching in the district. When I left the office I don't remember being particularly upset angry. I was used to being turned down, stared at, and feeling unwelcomed, because of the color of my skin. I was angry at racism and having to live under the conditions of what it means to be a Negro in this country.

Introspection

This black versus white thing was embedded in my brain, which sucked into it all the conditions and attitudes that those colors produced. Could my brain be reflecting a condition of inferiority? Could this separate housing conditions, the name-calling, the looks, and white people's overall mistreatment of black people have caused my brain to develop an inferiority complex?

It took me until college to figure out what was causing my perspiration attacks and my general discomfort in certain situations. I began to read, study, and work at ridding my brain of all those years of black versus white conditioning that can cause one to develop feelings of inferiority when dealing with white people in America. I began to read and study black history, which included American slavery, Jim Crow, racial segregation, and discrimination. I read about Frederick Douglass and George Washington Carver, Nat Turner and Harriet Tubman, W.E.B. Du Bois, Booker T. Washington, Dr. Drew, and all the great black leaders and contributors in American history who were never mentioned at any time during my education to that point.

During my senior year at San Diego State, as a member of the campus Wesley Foundation, I joined with other members to form a small group to speak to youth church groups on the topic of race relations. I was the only black person in the group. I decided that my speech would always be on self esteem, explaining how self-esteem among blacks can be damaged by the cruelty of racism.

After graduating from San Diego State College, I joined with a small group to form the African-American Association, whose purpose was to study and teach about the plight of black Americans. I also joined with a small interracial group to form a local chapter of the Congress of Racial Equality.

Study, reading, and discussion showed me the many accomplishments of black Americans and the courage and sacrifices they made to overturn slavery, and their fight against great odds to defeat the cruel system of white racism.

I became a black man long before we stopped calling ourselves Negro. I had succeeded in reconfiguring my brain to react to the black versus white words in a completely different way. Now my brain recognized that the only reason that the word black contained negative connotations was to place and keep economic and political power in the hands of people who are white. And my brain now understands that the negative connotations of the word black is for the purpose of making sure that black citizens are kept without any economic or political influence, after all, that is what controls our country.

I became a free man. My confidence and self-esteem began to grow. I became comfortable in any setting, social or otherwise. My brain was no longer brainwashed by white propagandists. I began to connect why Roy Rogers and Gene Autry, two white cowboys, wore white hats, and were the heroes who caught the crooks in the movie, and the white guys in the movie, who were the crooks, always wore black hats. That example is just one of many that took place as I became enlightened during my reading and studying of America's system of racism, and how color is used to obtain and control power for white America.

Speaking to CORE demonstrators at the Bank of America

CHAPTER THREE

CORE Beginnings

I continued as a full-time graduate student at SDSU after graduating in 1959. By this time my life was full of anger and hurt as a result of the many personal experiences I had with racism.

I know these personal experiences of mine were minuscule to what was happening all over the United States, especially in the South. But I was hurting inside, not only from my personal experiences with this horrible American color system, but from what I read and heard in the news: what seemed like countless incidents of violent and unfair treatment of people who looked like me.

There were lynching of blacks in the South and racial discrimination in employment, housing, and schools throughout the United States. People with my skin color suffered indignities at the hands of white people all over the country. Something had to be done to stop the physical and mental damage that was being inflicted on our people. I was tired of being treated as an inferior human being. I had no plans to do anything about trying to change things—I just knew it was time for me to do something. I concluded that this color monster and all the trouble it caused has to be wiped out, and I was going to do my part to help get rid of it.

My first effort in the fight to kill this color monster was to join a group called the El Cajon Open Housing Committee. I don't recall how I found out about this organization. It was an all-white group in El Cajon—a community just outside the city of San Diego. It was led by an energetic and articulate white woman by the name of Linda Storey, now Linda Navarro. The organization's purpose was to integrate housing in the El Cajon and La Mesa communities.

We went door-to-door with a petition asking homeowners to sign the petition stating that they would not object to living next door to a Negro. I don't recall getting anyone to sign the petition, but I do recall one man who came to the door and when I explained the petition to him and asked him if he would sign, he explained that the reason he moved there was because he wouldn't have to live next door to them. He shut the door and went back inside.

I remained a member of the group and attended other activities it sponsored until I met Jim Stone, a black man, who said that he wanted to form a San Diego chapter of the Congress of Racial Equality (CORE), and asked me if I was interested in joining the group.

I said yes, and he and I and a few others met a number of times to discuss the CORE organization and the requirements for forming a local chapter. Jim Stone turned out to be one of the most committed and dedicated people I have met during my whole experience of involvement in the civil rights struggle.

During the time we were holding meetings to discuss the formation of the local chapter, I was asked by some of the organizers to let them nominate me for the chairmanship position. I declined, informing them that I would participate as a member since I was starting my first year as a schoolteacher in the San Diego Unified

School District and I wanted to establish myself as a proficient teacher before I accepted the nomination to be the chairman.

My first participation in a civil rights demonstration was an uneasy experience. I felt very exposed and self-conscious. In the back of my mind, however, I understood it was a small price to pay given what this color monster was doing to destroy millions of lives. I knew the self consciousness was a temporary thing.

The first year of our chapter was spent picketing stores that had no black employees or employees of color. Our chapter was formed by a small group of us—black and white, all college educated professionals except Jim Stone.

At the end of my first year as a teacher, I was selected by the district as one of the top five outstanding first-year teachers in the district, so I felt I had established myself and could not easily be fired because of my civil -rights involvement. So when it was time for the election of officers for our second year, I was nominated for the chairmanship and I accepted the nomination.

I ran for chairman on a platform of black pride, self-determination, and aggressive action against racial discrimination and segregation. The idea of black pride and self-determination were concepts that were too progressive for some of the members at that time. This was the period of the early 1960s when integration of the races was the acceptable goal, while the term black pride and self-reliance were too threatening for many.

The word "black" itself, when referring to a Negro, was distasteful to most blacks and whites at that time. The word "Negro" was the preferred name for citizens of African descent.

Interestingly, in later years, the nation's African American community experienced a tremendous uplifting of black pride. Afro hairstyles and African attire were worn with pride and the words "black is beautiful" spread throughout the United States and reflected the feeling of most Negroes that they no longer felt that the color of their skin was a badge of dishonor—something to be ashamed of—as the government and many whites wanted Negroes to believe.

As we continued our chapter activities of investigating stores and companies where no blacks were employed, we learned that the President of the United States, John F. Kennedy, was coming to San Diego to speak at San Diego State University. There was to be a motorcade down El Cajon Boulevard. Our chapter decided that this would be a good opportunity to let the President know that we and our supporters were not going to tolerate San Diego's racial discrimination and segregation of its Negro citizens.

So, the day of the president's motorcade we placed ourselves at a spot on the motorcade route with signs that sent our message to President Kennedy that racial prejudice and discrimination existed right here in San Diego as it did in the South. We held our signs high and sang our freedom songs for the President and all others to see and hear.

The news media covered our demonstration, guaranteeing a wider audience than the president. We never knew what effect, if any, our demonstration had on President Kennedy and those who accompanied him, but we were compelled to speak out about San Diego's deplorable treatment of its Negro citizens. No one else in

San Diego was speaking out and we did not want President Kennedy to leave San Diego thinking that those conditions did not exist in "sunny and beautiful" San Diego.

After our demonstration I was asked by Channel 10 TV reporter Harold Keane to come to the station for an interview to explain why CORE demonstrated against the president. I accepted the invitation and explained that we did not demonstrate against the president: we demonstrated against San Diego's racial discrimination against its Negroes.

I watched the news cast at home. After my interview, the news station ran a story featuring a local prominent black minister, who proceeded to tell Keane and the audience that he did not agree with CORE's demonstration and did not support it.

As I listened to the minister's words I realized that my pledge to myself to work toward killing the color monster was going to be even more difficult than I realized. I knew there would be opposition to our fight, but I didn't expect that the opposition to come from some in the black community. I was crushed and angry. His words, I felt, were encouraged by some leaders in the white community and aimed at undermining CORE.

The minister lived in a black segregated neighborhood, was pastor of a black congregation, and saw the same racial injustices as I saw, but he spoke publicly against CORE's demonstration. I couldn't help but ask myself the question "even if he disagreed with our demonstration, why would he go on television and say that, for all of San Diego to hear?"

I remember going to bed after watching the minister's TV interview and spending a sleepless night thinking about how powerful this color monster must be to cause a black minister to denounce an organization's efforts to express the feelings of those who oppose the racial discriminatory practices in San Diego, which affected every member of his congregation.

I guess I should not have been surprised; during those years, the churches in San Diego were not speaking out against racial discrimination and segregation, and did not participate in or express any support of CORE's activities. However, there were two black ministers who individually supported CORE's demonstrations and at times participated in our picketing. One of them would attend some of our meetings. They were such an inspiration to me.

Black ministers are greatly respected by blacks. All my efforts to attempt to involve the black churches and ministers in CORE's efforts had little success. Churches in the black communities are the strongest and most organized part of the black community and we wanted them to support us. At one point I asked one prominent minister if I could meet with him and he agreed. I went to his home and we talked. He was quite a bit older than me and I felt that he was wondering what this kid wants from me. We had a nice discussion and he was very cordial, but he was not encouraging or supportive. I wanted him to know that I was not some crazy, radical kid, and that CORE was not some radical, irresponsible organization. My attempt to win his support was a not successful.

I was later severely criticized by a few CORE members for meeting with the minister. I had not informed anyone that I was going to meet with him. But that was part of the job as chairman, to speak with groups and talk with individuals to solicit their support for CORE.

There was one other time when I and the other members were disappointed in the behavior of our black ministers. We in CORE decided to express our anger with the city and the country's racism by organizing a protest march. About 200 of us gathered in front of our office on Imperial Avenue and began our march to the San Diego County Administration Building on Pacific Highway and Harbor Drive. It was a nice sunny day and we were all feeling good about the march and what we were trying to say to the city and county leaders of San Diego. We sang our freedom songs as we walked through the streets of our city toward the County Administration building.

I led the songs through the use of our bull horn, and we sang and walked and sang and walked through the hot sun to express our concerns to the mayor and the other city and county leaders, who all were white.

When we were about two blocks away from the county administration building, we suddenly stopped on the street leading to the county building and we could not believe our eyes. We saw the mayor and a group of black ministers standing with the mayor to receive our complaints about racial discrimination and segregation in San Diego. They were standing there as though they were not a part of the black community, but instead a part of the "power structure" that was responsible for the racial conditions that we protesting against. We were disgusted and angry to witness such a sight.

Some of our members wanted to take the bull horn and shout their anger toward the ministers who let themselves be used in such a manner. We were in shock because we had no idea that the black ministers were going to be there, much less standing with the perpetrator and defender of the racial practices in San Diego, to receive our complaints. I know it wasn't all of the black ministers in San Diego, but it was a large group.

Despite my anger, and knowing how angry the other members were, I would not allow anyone to use the bullhorn to "blast" the ministers. It was not the thing to do. I used the bull horn to address our members. I don't remember what I said, but I'm sure my anger and disgust were expressed. I did not feel that publicly attacking the ministers would help our cause or would it bring us any closer to winning the support of the black churches.

I don't remember what happened after we left the administration building, I only know I felt numb and disgusted— but not defeated. We all went home and lived to fight another day. I never heard anything from any of the ministers afterward.

Mentally I was depressed, but I was also angry. I was not going to let the CORE members know that my spirits were very low. I felt it was my responsibility as the chairman, to motivate and inspire the CORE members and our supporters to keep on fighting, and that we did.

Our CORE chapter was a small group of young, committed volunteer citizens. How could we defeat a system of color segregation

"Action At The Bank of America"

GOOD LUCK HAL	GOOD LUCK HAL	BEST WISHES & GOOD
Carrol Service Station	Mullen's Drive-In Liquor Store	LUCK IN YOUR
2717 Imperial Avenue	3011 Imperial Avenue	NEW ADVENTURE
	BE 4-9437	
Eddie Barnette, Owner	Robert Mullen	Jack Strum

Me with bullhorn leading demonstrations at Bank of America

and discrimination that apparently was supported and accepted by most Americans? Our chapter began to grow in number, but was still small. We continued to investigate companies and collect information about the number of employees, their job titles, and the color of their skin. We would obtain this information as best we could since our requests to companies for that information were ignored.

My being released from the county jail

It was CORE's policy nationally to submit a written request for information first. The second step was to request a meeting with the company to discuss our findings and attempt to resolve any issues we might have. The third step was to take direct action against the company in the form of picketing, sit-ins, marches, and other activities to draw public attention to the grievances we had against the company.

One of our chapter's concerns was with chain grocery stores. Our investigation of the stores found that there were no Negroes hired in any of these stores, not even in bagging groceries positions. While we were investigating companies in San Diego, CORE chapters throughout the United States were engaged in the same or similar activities with grocery store chains. It was very encouraging to know that across America, blacks and whites had enough of this

"Taking On The City"

Me speaking at CORE rally at County Administration Building and at Bank of America

"More Action At the Bank of America"

Me with others picketing at Bank of America

color craziness that was causing all these racial problems, and they were taking corrective action as we were in San Diego.

Of course it wasn't only CORE that was taking on the color monster. Throughout America there was the Student Nonviolent Coordinating Committee, the National Association for the Advancement of Colored People (NAACP), the Southern Christian Leadership Conference (SCLC), the Urban League, the Nation of Islam, and black and white university students: all of them, taking on this color monster that divided America since African slaves were forcefully brought to this country.

I was happy to be a part of this movement. It was inspiring to know that so many others were deeply upset and concerned about this color thing and committed to doing something about it.

Besides grocery stores, our chapter attempted to eliminate racial discrimination in hiring at local banks, the utility company, the San Diego Zoo, the San Diego Union Evening Tribune, and other local companies, as well as eliminate housing segregation in San Diego, which was practiced by the San Diego Realtors Association. This was a large undertaking for a small group such as ours. Many believed that we would not be able to do anything about it.

To add to the challenge, we were all volunteers and had no paid staff; we even lacked part-time employees. We were a group of mostly professional people with full-time jobs who came together after our workday was over to meet and discuss our plans and strategies to continue the fight.

And a fight it was. It was the small group of us against all those who were against what we stood for, and those who agreed with us but could not or would not participate with us for whatever reasons. So we continued to push forward our demand for equality in the hiring of Negroes, and the elimination of segregated housing in San Diego. Our efforts led us to many confrontations with those who disagreed with our goals or disagreed with our methods to accomplish them.

In the middle of taking on the responsibility of leading a local civil rights organization and fighting to remove the conditions caused by San Diego's racism, another wonderful thing happened to me. I became the father of another boy. Stephen Kent Brown was born on December 29, 1962. Steve became an outstanding student, developed as an outstanding basketball player and was recruited by Stanford University where he played basketball until he graduated. He later obtained a Master's Degree in Business Administration at the Kellogg Graduate School of Management at Northwestern University, Evanston Illinois. He has held several management positions in the technology industry and is currently a General Partner with Telegraph Hill Capital, a venture capital firm. He met his wife Marisa when they were students at Stanford University. She is an executive at Apple Computer, Inc., and today they are parents of McKenna, a senior at the University of California at Davis, and Elijah, a senior in high school.

Being a parent made my involvement in the civil rights movement even more important. If the conditions facing blacks had

My sons Michael and Stephen at our home

not changed, how could I face my children when they become old enough to ask me why we didn't try to change things?

Being the chairman of the San Diego chapter of CORE took on a life of its own. To me it meant taking on a tremendous amount of responsibility and risk, a responsibility that I took very seriously.

The chairman needed to provide the leadership that brought people together to fight for a common cause through non violent actions. The chairman needed to be able to show strength, but also compassion and sensibility, and be able to intelligently argue the cause for which we were fighting. The chairman needs to be forceful without appearing to be violent. We were already viewed by many as radicals. It was very important that the chairman not do anything that would embarrass black people. I can't say that I was aware of these things when I became chairman, but I think I intuitively knew that these were black people's expectations of the chairman.

The chairman also needed to be able to clearly articulate to the public the issues of racial discrimination and segregation in San Diego and throughout the nation and its effect on San Diego's citizens—both black and white. Our core chapter was not a large chapter. Although our membership dues were only $25 annually, our membership was usually around 50 people, although we would have about 200 at some of our marches.

However, it was not about numbers. I am reminded of the words of Dr. Margaret Mead, a great American Cultural Anthropologist, who said "Never Doubt That a Small Group of Thoughtful, Committed Citizens Can Change the World, Indeed It's the only Thing That Ever Has." Those were some of the words that guided me and gave me strength throughout my participation in the civil rights movement.

Most difficult, being the chairman required providing leadership that reflected the understanding of a people who has suffered through centuries of atrocious physical and mental abuse. At the time, I did not understand the serious impact the mental abuse had on our people. Later I came to understand the psychology of American racism and the psychological damage aimed at black America.

This was a time-consuming responsibility that took many after-work hours to plan our projects, which included gathering information on companies, attempting to meet with company representatives, developing our demands for change, and taking whatever direct actions that needed to be taken. There were many meetings that took place in the evenings after work hours and on Saturdays.

Our meetings, which I chaired, consisted of committee reports of the information gathered on the companies we were studying to obtain information regarding their number of employees, the racial designation of each employee, and the employee's job title. Reports were also given about San Diego's racially segregated housing practices, where certain areas of the city were set aside where blacks were forced to live. These reports were discussed and the projects we undertook were decided based on the amount of information we were able to obtain.

In many cases, we had to stand outside the businesses and visually count the people as they came to work, the only way we could obtain the information since the businesses refused to give it to us. When we decided which businesses we were going to take on as our project, we would develop our plan and strategy of negotiations and direct action against the racial discriminatory practices of the business we targeted.

Included in some of our meetings was role playing as antagonists and resistors to learn what it was like if we were confronted. The "antagonists" would heckle and call names such as "nigger" and "nigger lover." We would push and hit and shove each other to acquaint the demonstrators with what they might have to endure as a demonstrator. Each demonstrator had to pledge that he or she would not retaliate to any action of violence directed at us. That pledge was never broken at any of our demonstrations.

Also at our meetings we sang freedom songs that we sang during our demonstrations. These songs inspired us and gave us energy as we marched, picketed, and sat in. These songs also kept us focused on why we were there and what we were trying to accomplish.

I have great respect for that small group of citizens, the members and associate members of CORE, and those who joined our demonstrations in support of our mission. They, and I, faced strong opposition to our attempt to remove the racial segregation and discrimination practices in San Diego. They deserve the highest form of recognition, praising their courage, their sacrifice and commitment to easing the inhumane, unjust treatment of Negroes and others who did not have white skin.

CHAPTER FOUR

Energy for Change

What were the conditions in San Diego at the time CORE was founded? First, understand that San Diego CORE's demonstrations in the 1960s were not the first racial protest demonstrations held in San Diego.

According to Robert Fikes Jr's article, *The Struggle for Equality in America's Finest City: A History of the San Diego NAACP*, in 1927 the San Diego NAACP scored its first civil rights victory. It won the admittance of black women as nurses in the San Diego County Hospital. This was done under the leadership of the San Diego branch president, Elijah J. Gentry, a shoe shiner by trade (3).

According to Mr. Fikes, Mr. Gentry sent a frank assessment of the racial climate in San Diego to NAACP field secretary James Weldon Johnson in New York. Mr. Gentry wrote "colored people in San Diego are not allowed in restaurants, nor to drink soda water in drugstores, nor can they rent bathing suits at any bathing house or beach in this city" (Fikes 3).

Mr. Fikes' brief history goes on to state that "despite the small number of blacks in the area and the perception of racial tolerance, San Diego was nonetheless a very prejudiced city" (3). The webiste BlackPast's article, "A Brief History of the San Diego NAACP, 1917-2007" further states that "moreover, American-style racism had crept south of the border. In 1926 when branch officials looked across the border in Tijuana Mexico they saw signs in shops that proclaimed Colored Not Wanted."

The San Diego branch of the NAACP was founded in 1919. Over the years it produced some local chapter presidents who fought diligently to overcome San Diego's racial barriers. One of those people, Dr. Jack Kimbrough, a dentist, was president of the San Diego branch in 1947 and 1948.

According to Fikes:

> Dr. Kimbrough, having been refused a snack at a downtown greasy spoon, methodically devised a plan for redress that made him a pioneer in anti-discrimination protest tactics. At the dawn of the civil rights revolution he recruited a group of black and white students at San Diego State College, carefully rehearsed them to act as customers and witnesses and then targeted white owned restaurants that discriminated. As the black students were denied service, the already seated white students would observe what transpired and be prepared to testify in court as to what they had witnessed. Using Kimbrough's innovative scheme, the NAACP filed and won 31 of its 32 lawsuits against San Diego restaurants in little over a year, usually with court awards to plaintiffs of $300 per case, which was split between the students and their attorney. Kimbrough followed up this trial with the desegregation of the Grant Grill at the prestigious US Grant Hotel in downtown San Diego in 1948. (5)

"A Brief History of the San Diego NAACP, 1917-2007" states that "in 1946 the San Diego branch membership stood at 1,803." By

1951, the San Diego chapter's membership had declined to only 240, and the branch had to face the issue of being accused of having members of the Communist Party as members of their branch. This accusation was a tactic used by those who were enemies of civil rights organizations (BlackPast).

When I graduated from college in 1959, I tried to join the San Diego branch of the NAACP, but after numerous telephone calls and visits to their office, I was unable to contact anyone to obtain information as to how to become a member. I finally gave up trying. Mr. Fikes' article states that sometime in the early 1950s, the San Diego NAACP was placed on the bureaucratic equivalent of life support; the national office declared it "inactive."

The NAACP did a great job in trying to grapple with this racial problem in San Diego. But, of course the racial problems continued and were far from being solved and needed others to continue the fight.

In 1959, while participating with the El Cajon open housing committee, I met Jim Stone, a black man whom I would come to respect as one of the most committed people that I had the pleasure of working with in the San Diego civil rights movement. Jim asked me if I was interested in helping to form a San Diego chapter of the Congress of Racial Equality, CORE, and I replied yes. I had not heard of CORE, so Jim explained that it was one of the major civil rights organizations in America. At that time, there was no sign of any organized effort to address the racial problems in San Diego, with two exceptions: the Afro-American Association, led by Josh von Wolfolk, of which I was a member, and Chollas Democratic Club.

Von Wolfolk was a black man who had a deep understanding of the plight of the Negro in America. The purpose of the Afro-American Association was to study, learn, and teach about that plight. The group studied Negro history together and held speaking sessions and small rallies at Mountain View Park on Sunday afternoons. The other organization, Chollas Democratic Club, led by Ted Patrick, aimed its efforts at addressing police brutality and job discrimination against the Negro. So, in 1960, Jim Stone and a small group of us formed the San Diego chapter of the Congress of Racial Equality (CORE).

We began our attack on racial segregation and discrimination and continued the fight started by the NAACP in 1919. We directed our efforts toward eliminating total and widespread racial injustices in housing, employment, and education in San Diego.

The total population of San Diego in 1960 was a little over one million. The black population was at 6.7 percent and most blacks lived in the southeastern section of San Diego. The practice was to keep blacks confined to housing in certain areas of the city. This was enforced and maintained through the use of "restrictive covenants" where whites signed to agree that they would not rent or sell their house or apartment to a Negro.

As explained by the Fair Housing Center of Greater Boston: racially restrictive covenants refer to contractual agreements that prohibit the purchase, lease, or occupation of a piece of property by a particular group of people, usually African Americans. Racially restrictive covenants were not only mutual agreements between property owners in a neighborhood, but were also agreements enforced through the cooperation of real estate boards and neighborhood associations. Racially restrictive covenants became common after 1926 after the U.S. Supreme Court decision, Corrigan v. Buckley, which validated their use.

The racially restrictive covenants were used nationwide to prevent people of color from purchasing homes in white communities. The covenants were an important and fundamental part of the color monster disease, and were used to maintain segregation in America. This practice, of course, produced segregated schools.

The partner of housing segregation was, then, employment discrimination. Companies in San Diego offered few jobs to Negroes, except for those companies which had government contracts and were guided by federal contracts to hire minorities. Food markets, clothing stores, banks, insurance companies, car dealerships, financial companies, San Diego Zoo, hotels, and many more did not hire Negroes. Our CORE chapter found that blacks could not even get jobs as tellers in banks or baggers in grocery stores.

No one was speaking out on these issues in San Diego. The last time racial discrimination in San Diego was challenged was when Woolworth Department Store was picketed by a group that was led by Dr. Jack Kimbrough, a prominent black dentist. The group challenged Woolworth's policy of not serving Negroes at its lunch counters.

Most of the job market in San Diego was essentially closed to Negroes other than in Southeast San Diego. Most black school teachers taught there, Medical doctors and lawyers also had offices there. Only one lawyer had his practice outside Southeast San Diego. His office was located in the downtown area at Horton Plaza.

Another time when the color monster made its presence known to me was when I graduated from San Diego State College with a degree and a California teaching credential. Since I was living in La Mesa, a city just on the edge east of San Diego, I went to the office of the La Mesa Spring Valley School District to apply for a teaching position. I was politely told by the man who interviewed me that they would have to get the approval of the parents living in the district to see if they would object to having a Negro teaching in their district. I never expected such a response and I don't remember what my response was or how the conversation ended. However, I was more angry than surprised. Most black persons living in San Diego knew that the cities just east of San Diego were worst racially for blacks than they were in San Diego. Jobs for blacks were practically non-existent east of San Diego, in the areas like La Mesa, El Cajon, and Lakeside.

In 1960, CORE decided to challenge San Diego's way of life in its discriminatory treatment of Negro citizens. These discriminatory practices were accepted, and thereby supported by the mayor, city council members, board of supervisors, churches, businesses and civic groups. Even though citizens around the United States were protesting against the same conditions that existed in San Diego, there were no actions being taken in San Diego by any group to address this disastrous treatment of the Negro, other than the Afro-American Association and the Chollas Democratic Club.

San Diego CORE, with its small membership of black and white members, dedicated itself to following National CORE's rules of investigation, mediation, and nonviolent direct action. One of our first actions, as far as I can remember, was to organize a picket line at the parade for President John Kennedy who was in San Diego to speak at San Diego State College. The purpose of the picketing was to express to the President and make him aware that there were deplorable racial conditions in San Diego. We later directed our efforts toward the not hiring of Negroes at grocery stores, and at other places where Negroes were not employed, such as the San Diego Zoo, the San Diego Union newspaper, the San Diego Gas & Electric Company, the banks and other financial companies.

Actions against San Diego Gas & Electric Company (SDG&E) produced our first arrests. Our meetings with SDG&E officials produced no results in the hiring of Negroes. SDG&E refused to admit that it discriminated against Negroes and took no action to attempt to hire any. After one of our meetings with SDG&E representatives, I felt that we were making some progress. However, when I returned home and watched the news on television, I was shocked to listen to SDG&E representatives paint a very negative picture of CORE. This angered and disappointed me greatly, so I stayed up most of the night writing counter arguments to the remarks made by the SDG&E representatives. We then began to take direct action against SDG&E in the form of picketing and sit-ins. We picketed in front of their offices for months and we conducted sit-ins inside their main office.

As we picketed outside their main office during the Christmas holiday season, we decided to dress one of our members, who had dark skin, in a Santa Claus Uniform and put him on the picket line. We felt it would be a good idea to introduce San Diegans to the idea of Santa Claus not only being white—and have some fun doing it. We enjoyed watching the heads of people who drove by, snap their heads around, and stretch to see if they saw what they just saw, a black Santa Claus? No way! This was our attempt to strike a blow against the color monster while at the same time striking a blow against SDG&E's discriminatory hiring practices.

SDG&E then filed a lawsuit against us to limit the number of CORE demonstrators that were allowed to picket in front of their building, at any one time, to three or four people. While I don't recall the exact number, I remember it was small and that it was ridiculous. I stated in my remarks to the CORE membership that any law that limited to a minimal expression of any group working to eliminate racial discrimination in the workplace, makes this group's expression unheard. So, after discussing it at our next meeting we decided to ignore the lawsuit and continued to picket. Ignoring the lawsuit meant that if we exceeded the number of picketers that the lawsuit allowed, all those who were picketing would be arrested. Limiting the number who could picket at the same time to three or four people was obviously SDG&E's attempt to lower or eliminate the visibility of our protest and thereby weaken our message to the general public about their refusal to hire Negroes. Police came, arrested all six or seven of us, and took us to jail. We were bailed out the same day.

CORE member Jim Stone, dressed in Santa Claus suit at San Diego Gas & Electric Company

Based on the information that we received from one of SDG&E's employees, there was only one black person employed at SDG&E when we began our demonstrations against them. Later during one of our demonstrations, we saw that there was a black man seated at one of the desks in their office. We assumed that the company had hired a second black employee.

One day during our demonstrations against SDG&E, a white man showed up with a picket sign to protest against our picketing of SDG&E. He was alone and carried a sign with a message written on it, but I don't remember what the message was. A few days later when I read the *Voice Newspaper*, a newspaper serving the black community, there was a story covering our picketing at SDG&E. The newspaper's coverage included a photo of the person picketing against CORE with a caption under the photo identifying the person as a member of the Nazi Party. This person filed a lawsuit against the Voice Newspaper and against CORE charging the newspaper and CORE with Slander and Defamation of his Character.

The *Voice Newspaper* hired a lawyer to defend it and somehow I ended up being the person to defend CORE. Our chapter did not have the money to pay for a lawyer and the lawyers who were providing our legal defense pro bono were not available. So, since I was the chairman and spokesperson for CORE, it fell on me to be the one to defend CORE in this legal matter. I was not a lawyer, had never been to law school, and I was not exactly sure what slander and defamation of character really meant legally. So, I spent time at the law library studying about slander and defamation.

The time came to appear in Court and the trial began. I paid close attention to how the lawyer for the Voice Newspaper and the plaintiff's lawyer were handling the case and I felt comfortable representing CORE. During the selection of the jury I questioned each potential juror and accepted or dismissed the potential juror based on the answers to my questions. When the trial ended, CORE and the *Voice Newspaper* were found not guilty.

As the trial ended, the judge said to me, "Mr. Brown, have you ever gone to law school?" I replied, "no, your honor." The judge then said, "you presented the case as well as some lawyers who come before me." That was enough ego food to last me for a year.

As I mentioned earlier, I was a schoolteacher in the San Diego Unified School District while leading CORE. I taught school each day and did CORE work after my work day ended.

One day in 1963, not long after the demonstrations against SDG&E, I received a subpoena from a National Republican Subcommittee requiring me to appear before the subcommittee to provide testimony as to why CORE was holding demonstrations against SDG&E.

The committee held the meeting in San Diego, and I was told to bring all CORE materials to the meeting. I notified my school principal of the subpoena, and I attended the subcommittee's meeting, carrying a couple boxes of CORE's records and materials. As best I can recall, the meeting lasted all day for a couple of days. I remember being discouraged and frustrated by the naïve questions and conservative remarks from the members of the committee. I attended the meeting alone. There were no CORE members and no CORE attorneys to support my testimony. I remember feeling very lonely, as well as angry. I don't know why I didn't try to have others attend the meeting with me. I guess it was because the meeting lasted all day and most CORE members were at work, or that it just did not occur to me to have others attend. I felt I could handle whatever would come up. Besides, I did not want to inconvenience others by asking them to spend all day sitting at a meeting and not knowing when I would be called to give my testimony. As I look back I realize that I should have asked the members to attend if they could. I am sure some of the members would have attended. On the other hand, I am not sure that visitors were allowed to attend the meeting.

During the remarks by one of the members of the committee, I became so frustrated and angry at his remarks that during the lunch break I went home and grabbed my book titled *100 Years of Lynching*. I raced back the meeting and walked up to where the person was seated and slammed the book in front of his microphone, and said to him, "you need to read this!" That made me feel better, albeit temporarily. Later in the meeting, an SDG&E executive testified that SDG&E did not discriminate against Negroes. He explained the reason the company did not have Negro employees was because workers needed to climb poles where wires were attached, and Negroes were afraid of heights. That statement was typical of the resistance we received from SDG&E. Another person who testified before the committee on behalf of SDG&E told the committee members that the way the company filled its vacant positions was to post the vacant positions on the company's bulletin boards which hung on the walls inside the company. "So, SDG&E did not discriminate against Negroes." Obviously, if you don't have Negroes working in your company, and you only advertise your job openers to the current employees who all are white, chances are your company will never have any Negroes employees. To us in CORE it sounded like a pretty sure way of keeping Negroes out.

These were examples that represented the resistance we received from San Diego's mayor, Frank Kern, and Police Chief Wesley Sharp. The Mayor stated at a private meeting that a few of us

CORE members had with him during the SDG&E demonstrations that he saw no need for CORE's demonstrations. He then made a number of, what I felt were pious statements, that revealed his lack of understanding of the racial problems in San Diego, and I stated that in the meeting. Another example of the mayor's insensitivity was when he and I and a few others were invited to be on a panel to appear on television to discuss San Diego's race relations problems, the Mayor shouted that he would not allow race riots in San Diego. This program was produced by the three main TV channels 10, 8, and 6, and was aired by the three stations on the same day at the same hour. The mayor's remarks, I assumed to be a reaction to the 1965 Watts Riots in Los Angeles. This of course was an outrageous statement made out of ignorance regarding the racial problem in San Diego. I replied to the Mayor's ridiculous words with a shout of my own: "You can't stop people from rioting!" I had heard enough of his pious and threatening statements.

Further evidence of San Diego's response to the racial issue at that time was reported by Jim Miller. He was one of the authors of the book entitled *Under the Perfect Sun*. He stated that Harold Keen, in his article "San Diego's Racial Powder Keg" for San Diego Magazine, that there was skepticism on the part of those in local government and in the Chamber of Commerce as to whether the city even had a problem with racial discrimination. In *Under the Perfect Sun*, Jim Miller also pointed out that some black San Diego leaders agreed with CORE about the racial problem in San Diego.

He quoted Rev. Dwight Kyle, Pastor of Bethel African Methodist Episcopal Church as saying that San Diego in 1963 was the worst place on the coast in racial discrimination practices. Mr. Miller also wrote that Hartwell Ragsdale, then president of the San Diego chapter of the National Association for the Advancement of Colored People, "complained about racial discrimination within the labor movement" (221). The book also quotes me as saying "through the years, no substantial steps were taken by the white leaders out of their own consciences. They had to be pushed and if we must hold demonstrations to obtain what is long past due, we will demonstrate" (221). And we did.

Picketing continued at SDG&E during the Christmas holiday season, with our black Santa Claus in tow. In spite of a lot of white opposition and little black participation, we continued picketing and demonstrating against housing and employment discrimination. Those who participated can be proud of the results. Looking at SDG&E since the end of the 1960s, we see a very different company. Blacks and other non-whites are employed in positions throughout the company. Recently, SDG&E had a black person as its Chairman and CEO. The company learned and opened its doors of employment to everyone. It's a beautiful sight to see that it has many employees of different ethnic backgrounds and cultures, and employment is not based on the color of one's skin. This was accomplished without the shedding of one drop of blood or one act of physical violence. It was accomplished because a small group of committed and dedicated citizens felt that they "could change the world."

CHAPTER FIVE

Banking on Equality

During the mid 1960s, National CORE, under the leadership of Founder and National Director Jim Farmer, modified the organization's structure and divided the organization into regions. Each region would have a chairman who would serve as a member of the National Action Council.

I was selected to serve as Chairman of the Western Region. My responsibility as Western Regional Chairman was to represent CORE chapters in the region on national policy issues and actions related to CORE's involvement in the civil rights movement. This responsibility called for me to attend regular National Action Council meetings at CORE's national office in New York City. These meetings were held monthly and more often during emergencies. I would take a red eye flight from San Diego to New York. The meetings were held starting early Saturday morning and lasted until late that night, and started again early Sunday morning. I would leave the meeting in time to catch my flight back to San Diego which would allow me to be at work Monday morning. Sometimes I attended those meetings twice in one month.

While this was physically demanding, it was not physically tiring. I was glad to be in a position where I could apply my energies toward destroying this color monster that has been used for hundreds of years to demean, brutalize, and destroy an entire people. It was no time to be tired.

We had to keep fighting, no matter what the odds were against us. We owed it to those who came before us, whose shoulders we stood on and who fought to get us this far, many losing their lives along the way. We felt that we owed it to our children and all who would come after us. I didn't want my children to have to go through life being subjected to this country's racial treatment of its black citizens. Besides, what a great experience it was to be among such great, wonderful, highly intelligent, committed human beings, black and white, female and male, who were fighting to rid this country of racism, just like we were doing in San Diego. It was a privilege to serve on the National Action Council (NAC) with Jim Farmer, our national director, Floyd McKissick, our national chairman, and the other NAC members. The NAC gave direction and support to the local chapters and was there for help whenever needed.

Bank of America Project

After the SDG&E project ended, CORE took on Bank of America (B of A). The idea to take on the banks, and attack their racial discriminatory practice against Negroes, came from the San Francisco CORE chapter. This chapter, led by its Chairman Bill Bradley, decided that they wanted this to be a region wide action against B of A. Bill discussed the idea with me as the regional chairman, and I thought it was a great idea.

Bill and his chapter took the lead. He organized the project and we called upon all of the chapters in California to participate. Our San Diego chapter participated fully and was one of the most, if not the most, active chapter involved in the project. Since Bank of America was the largest bank in California, it made sense that if we could pry open its doors to hire Negroes and other people of color, we could expect the other banks to follow, as well as other companies. And since B of A was headquartered in San Francisco, Bill Bradley and his San Francisco chapter was the ideal leader for the project. The members and supporters of our San Diego chapter were eager to take on the banks where no Negroes were employed in San Diego.

In May, 1964, San Francisco CORE and the San Francisco chapter of NAACP organized the picketing of Bank of America to protest its discriminatory hiring practices. Our CORE chapter, after receiving no cooperation from B of A, began picketing the company's main office on Broadway Street. For many weeks we picketed, conducted sit-ins, and held marches and coin-ins. A coin-in consisted of protesters standing in line at each of the teller windows and asking for rolls of pennies, then breaking the rolls open and counting the rolls while standing at the teller's window. Or we would take a number of pennies to the teller's window and ask to exchange them for dollar bills, and count the pennies while standing at the teller's window. This was a tactic to produce long waiting lines to discourage customers from banking with B of A until the bank agreed to hire Negroes and other people of color throughout the state of California. Weeks and months went by as we continued our demonstrations in front of the bank's doors and in the bank's lobby. Our demonstrations attracted large numbers of supporters, black and white, who marched and picketed with us.

Bank of America would not talk with us, but they would end up calling one of the black ministers and ask for help in recruiting Negro employees. While the demonstrations were peaceful with speeches and lots of singing the freedom songs, there were two instances of violent reactions to our demonstrations.

One instance was when some of our protesters were physically attacked by a group of young white fellows. This could have developed into a major incident had it not been for the adherence to our nonviolent action and our pledge to not react to violence by committing violence. The young fellows pushed and grabbed some of those who were picketing, but I did not see anyone being knocked to the ground. Being the leader, I prepared myself to be hit. I was not hit or shoved. However, one of our members who was a high school wrestling coach, was shoved around pretty hard. As I watched, I thought "boy if they only knew that he was a wrestling coach..." and if this was not a nonviolent demonstration, they would be in serious trouble.

The other incident expressed more antagonism toward us when a bucket of feces was collected, mixed with water or urine, or both, and dumped on us out of the upper windows of the B of A building as we were picketing. We did not retaliate. We just kept on picketing and singing the words of one of our freedom songs, "Keep Your Eyes on The Prize, Hold on." I must admit that watching our demonstrators being hit and shoved around by those young white fellows angered me greatly, and I remember wishing that those fellows would attack me rather than our demonstrators. It was obvious that I was leading the demonstration, but they never touched me. As I recall, I only saw them attack the white demonstrators.

As we continued our protests, those of us who were sitting in, were told by the policeman in charge to remove ourselves from the premises or be placed under arrest. Those of us who refused to move were arrested while the couple hundred demonstrators stood in the street facing the B of A building singing along with those of us sitting in the lobby the words of one of the civil rights songs, "We Shall Not Be Moved," and another song "We Shall Overcome." We were charged with trespassing, booked, and taken to jail. Hours later we were bailed out by our CORE lawyers who provided their time and legal expertise pro bono. I was arrested for trespassing along with other members of CORE including Dr. Charles Collins, a dean at Grossmont College, his wife Ann Collins, and George Stevens, a long-time friend, whom I recruited to join CORE and who later became a member of the San Diego City Council.

At the time, there was much criticism of CORE. As Jim Miller pointed out in the book *Under the Perfect Sun*, CORE was condemned by then Mayor Frank Kern, members of the city council, judges, and police. Of course, much of the white community did not approve of our actions either. Also pointed out by Miller was that Dr. Collins' jailers at the county jail, who were white, made their racism readily apparent, calling the white academic a "nigger lover," and asking Dr. Collins if he would like his daughters to marry a couple of niggers. Dr. Collins told me that he replied to that question by telling

By HAROLD KEEN

● "They applaud the actions of civil rights workers in Mississippi, but in their own town they're treated like criminals."

Pouring out his resentment is a slender, soft-spoken Negro who in the black revolution of 1964 has emerged as the personal symbol of non-violent militancy that surged into streets and business establishments of San Diego in deliberate defiance of the law. Harold Brown is a 30-year-old physical education instructor at Einstein Junior High School, a former basketball star at San Diego State College, a home owner in a well-tended, middle-class, integrated neighborhood—an apparently well-provided Negro who has profited from the opportunities San Diego has afforded him.

He is also San Diego and Western Regional Chairman of the Congress of Racial Equality (CORE), and as such the object of mixed feelings in the community. His followers, white and Negro, consider him a rising civil rights leader cast in the mold of Dr. Martin Luther King. His critics, ranging from judges to jailers to street scoffers, embarrassed or angered by CORE demonstrations, avoid any philosophical essence of the civil rights struggle and view him simply as an outlaw.

As the central figure in a three-month string of lawsuits resulting in 27 convictions (the most severe penalties, 15 and 30-day jail terms, are under appeal) of CORE members for trespassing, business obstruction and violating court restraining orders, in the equal opportunity hiring conflict with the Bank of America, Brown r e j e c t s implications of irresponsible leadership. He has been so reproached, either directly or indirectly, by the Mayor, the Municipal Court bench and law enforcement officers. "We have been told, in effect, that responsible leadership consists of not rocking the boat," says Brown. "But this is exactly what we must do to correct ancient wrongs. San Diego may not be as bad as the South in the sense that a Negro is fearful for his life, but it is just as bad when it deprives a Negro of real dignity by discriminating and segregating, and making him a different part of the community. What do Whites mean when they say there is no segregation in San Diego? Look at Logan Heights, and look at schools whose enrollment is 95 per cent black. It is just as frustrating in San Diego as in the backwoods of Mississippi.

Above: San Diego's Harold Brown, Western Regional Chairman of CORE. "The Mayor has not shown deep concern about our problem."
Right: Grossmont College's Dr. Charles Collins and his wife. "Laws are not infallible."

WHY CORE BREAKS THE LAW

Me (top), CORE members Dr. Charles Collins and wife Ann Collins (bottom)

the jailer that it would be a much better choice than marrying the likes of him. Yes, animosity certainly was there among the jailers. I received a letter while in jail and my letter had the word "NIGGER" printed by hand across the front of the envelope.

Another example of the lack of understanding of racism by many in the white community was when I was interviewed by a white TV news reporter. She asked me why we were doing this, referring to our protest demonstrations. "Mr. Brown, why don't you spend your time volunteering for some organization like the American Heart Association or something like that?" Usually, I had a reply for most questions but I was unable to come up with an answer that I felt would adequately respond to such an ignorant and uninformed question. Another question that astounded me came from Harold Keen, a TV program host, while interviewing me on the subject of race relations in San Diego, he responded to my remarks with the question "but isn't it better here in San Diego than in Mississippi?" I thought of some choice words to respond to Harold's question, but I was on TV. Besides, I thought Harold meant well. He just had no real understanding of the depth of this problem in America.

Picketing continued for a while after the B of A arrests, but then B of A began to hire Negroes and other minorities at their branches throughout California. B of A then entered into an agreement with the State Fair Employment Practices Commission to implement equal employment opportunity policies and hire more people of color. This was a big victory for CORE and all non-white groups throughout California, and a victory for the national civil rights movement. Although the general public may not have been tuned in to CORE's B of A project, I'm sure the banking community was well aware. If we look at the B of A today, we will find a bank that has changed so dramatically in its hiring practices that it would be hard to believe that its hiring practices for the entire time of its existence until CORE's action, excluded Negroes and other people of color. Although the battle with B of A was a hard one, we decided to end the project, feeling that much had been accomplished. The battle was over. We had pushed open the doors of B of A and made available many jobs for those who had been shut out because of the color of their skin. We were confident that our battle with B of A had sent a message to all the other banks as well as to other businesses.

Now that the battle on the field was over, it was time for battle in the courts.

The CORE attorneys prepared the defense for those of us who were arrested by B of A on charges of trespassing. As a result of our protest demonstrations against their practice of refusing to hire Negroes and other people of color, we all were found guilty. I argued during my testimony that CORE's demonstrations were justified, and needed, to correct the long-standing practices of B of A, that denied employment to individuals who were not white. I cited the fact that because of our demonstrations, B of A began to hire non-white employees, even at the management level.

None of these arguments, or the arguments of my attorney, seemed to carry any weight with the prosecuting attorney or the judges that I faced. After being found guilty of the various charges against me, I received sentences totaling 125 days and served my days in jail on weekends. I was allowed to teach school during the week, and report to jail on Friday evenings. I was released on Sunday mornings to attend church. This was granted as result of the judge's approval of the request submitted by the attorney for George Stevens, who was another CORE member being sentenced. I reported back to jail after church and was released again on Sunday evening. At the end of serving all my jail time, Dr. Charles Collins, a CORE member, who served as our public relations chairman, issued the following news release:

> HAL BROWN PAYS DEBT TO SOCIETY: Hal Brown, Western Regional Director, has served all the time in jail to which he was sentenced for his leadership in the fair employment demonstrations against the Bank of America. Brown was sentenced 5 days by Superior Court Judge Vincent Whalen, 30 days by Municipal Court Judge Madge Bradley and 90 days by Municipal Court Judge Roy Fitzgerald. Each of the sentences had some jail time suspended but the total put the CORE leader behind bars almost every weekend during the last six months.
>
> After his final release from the County Jail, Brown stated: "A man has to do what his times and circumstances require him to do. I'm a Negro living in the period of the Negro revolt. I wouldn't want to be anywhere but on the front lines of this most necessary social revolution. The Bank of America put me in jail but the demonstrations which I led put Negroes working in the Bank of America. Jail is the tough price a man has to pay if he is going to be active in a non-violent revolution."
>
> Brown reported that he held no grudge against the Bank of America and was encouraged by what the top ranking bank officials were now saying. Brown quoted from a

speech by James F. Langton, Vice President of the Bank of America: "What should be the business response to the Negro Revolution? First, I think we must realize that what might be termed neutral equal opportunity programs are not enough, there must be some aggressive employment programs designed to seek out and encourage Negro applicants. Secondly, we must find some better way of communicating with the Negro community, and third, we must aggressively seek Negroes not only for our workforce but also for our management." Brown emphasized that even before the Los Angeles Watts riots, Langton had concluded his speech by saying: "New York's Harlem, Chicago's South Side, San Francisco's Hunter's Point-Fillmore and Los Angeles' Watts district are explosives awaiting a match. The only real question is whether we will provide the match or remove the explosive."

To honor Hal Brown and the others who served jail terms for local civil rights demonstrations, the San Diego Chapter of CORE will have a public party beginning at 8:00 P.M. on Friday, February 4, at the Loyal Buddies, Inc., 3638 Ocean Boulevard.

After serving my days in jail, I was completely exhausted and burned out. I was unable to sit in a meeting or take part in a conversation to discuss the race issue. My nervous system seemed unable to handle any more stress. The five years of serving as San Diego CORE's chairman, serving a term as CORE's Western Region Chairman, and doing my job as a schoolteacher, began to take its toll. I loved teaching school. I loved my students. I had a wonderful and very supportive principal at our school, Dr. Wayne Laughery, and I enjoyed my colleagues. I don't believe I ever let the civil rights movement and my involvement in it, interfere with teaching my students. I loved them and I felt they loved me. Perhaps teaching school was what allowed me to endure the stress of being a leader in the civil rights movement and the leader of San Diego CORE.

The Battle Within

Stress was not just the result of leading protest demonstrations. Stress came also from the in-fighting within our CORE chapter itself. By 1965, I felt tremendous stress as a result of a split in our chapter: one group attempting to oust me as the chairman, and the other group supporting me. Although the group attempting to oust me never voiced any specific charges against me, their anger, as I understood it, was centered on their assuming that I was opposed to having members of CORE who were members of the Communist and Trotskyist Parties. I never expressed whether I was or not, but our National CORE's Constitution prohibited it, and I was following the rules of our constitution.

Our meetings became extremely turbulent and very uncomfortable for me. Chairing these meetings was exhausting. I was never asked if I was personally opposed to having as CORE members those who were members of the Communist Party or the Trotskyist Socialist Party. I was opposed to any members of another group who were trying to take control of our chapter for the benefit of their group's ideals and philosophy, which were not consistent with CORE'S. I knew very little about the Communist

Party and nothing about the Trotskyist Party. What I did know was the Communist Party was unacceptable in America and to be called a Communist or a Communist sympathizer would label you as not being loyal to America. I was very much aware of what was known as the "red scare" in America during the 1950s when Senator Joseph McCarthy led the fight against Communism and labeled a number of Americans as "subversive," which caused them to lose their jobs. If one is accused of being a Communist or participating with a group that was accused of being sympathetic to Communism or the Trotskyist movement, could seriously damage CORE'S ability to attract members to its cause of breaking down the barriers of racial segregation and discrimination. The "red scare" was also used by white segregationists and others opposed to civil rights groups, for the purpose of discouraging potential members from joining civil rights groups such as CORE.

The group that was formed within our chapter took strong steps to remove me as the chairman. They wrote to National CORE submitting their complaints. National CORE sent a representative to our chapter to investigate the complaints. National CORE took no action.

After one of our evening meetings, it was dark outside when I left the meeting. I was walking to my car alone when two members of the group that was calling for my ouster, approached me in the parking lot. They stood there for a while talking and I could see they were very upset with me. We exchanged words of disagreement and they were extremely angry. During our conversation one of them put his hands on his belt inside his coat and said "Nigger, I'll blow your brains out." I then walked away and nothing was said or done to me.

These two men were black. I felt very lonely as I drove home that night, and I guess too tired to be afraid, And furthermore, my mother and my brothers and sisters had always taught me through their actions to not be afraid and how to fight. This was a valuable lesson they taught me, although they never knew it. So, I was not afraid. But then I was no fool either, I knew I could run faster than either of them. I was 26 years old when we formed the San Diego chapter of CORE and I was 27 when I became chairman.

Most of us who were in leadership positions as civil rights activists were waging a war on American racism without power, money, equipment, experience, or training in civil rights protest. Whenever I was criticized for something CORE did, I would remind the person that we did not have a training manual for civil rights activists, or "how-to" books we could read about tearing down the walls of discrimination and segregation. We only had the faith of God and the strength of each other. I think I can say now that it appears that was enough.

The stress from this encounter and the many turbulent meetings within our CORE chapter, made the words of the two songs we sang so many times during our civil rights marches and demonstrations—"Keep Your Eyes on the Prize, Hold On," and "Ain't Gonna Let Nobody Turn Me Around"—have a deeper meaning for me. The stress from my battle with the ousting group was tempered by the fact that I felt I had the support of most of our members and also the support of National CORE because of its Constitution. I felt the comfort of support from our national leader, Jim Farmer, with whom I worked on CORE's National Action Council (NAC), and the other members of the NAC, some who had experienced the same or similar problems that I was experiencing.

Through my contacts on the NAC, I learned that our CORE chapter was not the only chapter that was going through or had gone through a struggle with this communist and Trotskyist issue. I felt strongly that the race and color issue was more than enough for us to tackle. Taking on the issue of another ideology made no sense to me, even if you agreed with it. In fact, at my age I knew very little about communism and I was not interested in knowing anything about it. I did feel, however, that other groups wanted to use the civil rights movement to further their own cause, and I guarded against that happening in our chapter. I later learned that in the early years, after CORE was founded, some CORE chapters had a problem with Communists and Trotskyist becoming members of CORE and attempting to take over the chapter's leadership.

Another point of stress for me in addition to our turbulent meetings and trying to coexist with a conservative San Diego and racism in America, was trying to persuade a conservative black community to join us in the fight against San Diego's practice of racial discrimination and segregation. I guess I expected that more blacks would show their support of our goals, even if they disagreed with some of our tactics. Yes, there were some blacks who joined the civil rights movement in San Diego, but far too few. Did black San Diego support the actions of San Diego CORE? I believe most did, but only a small number expressed that support or participated. This was very discouraging. In spite of all my efforts, I was unable to get the San Diego branch of the NAACP, the San Diego Urban League, or the black churches to join us in the fight to remove the obstacles that prevented black men and women, and black children, from participating as full and equal citizens of San Diego. Our chapter did its best to attract new members. We sent out news releases and, our demonstrations were covered by the newspapers and television stations. I was a speaker at some of the organizations, and I wrote a column in the *Voice Newspaper* entitled "Speaking Out," asking for support of CORE's activities. The *Voice Newspaper*, now the *Voice and Viewpoint*, was a critical part of CORE's attack on racial discrimination in San Diego. Every movement needs a means to communicate its message. The Voice Newspaper provided that means and was a communication link to the black community.

Why was the participation from the black community so minimal? I can only speculate. I have given much thought to this question over the years and I can only conclude that fear of reprisals from whites was at the top of the list. It is easy for me to understand that fear. To know or strongly believe that your job, your promotion, or the possibility of not being considered for a position you had your eyes on, would be in jeopardy if it was known that you supported a "radical militant" organization such as CORE. Of course CORE was not a radical organization, but some wanted the public to believe that is was. Black people knew very well that San Diego was a conservative city, and the city fathers did not look favorably on anyone who would rock the boat and cause trouble, and CORE was rocking the boat.

Challenging San Diego's racial discrimination and segregation was "causing trouble" for many in the white community and especially for San Diego's leadership. We in CORE were labeled as radicals, communists, militants, and trouble makers. This may be one of the reasons why only a small number of blacks participated with or showed support of CORE. Also, CORE was an organization that practiced non-violence, which meant that we would not use violence to achieve our goals, even if violence was used against us, and many blacks were not going to, as one black man said to a group of people, "I'm not going to let white folks hit and knock me to the ground and call me nigger and not fight back."

Being a civil rights activist during the 1960s in San Diego was not fashionable or respected. Some blacks felt that we civil rights activists were only making conditions worst for them. Participating in an organization led by a young schoolteacher who was not a doctor or a minister, I believe, was also part of the list of things that kept most San Diego blacks from participating with us. Then there was the Communist and Trotskyist issue. To what extent blacks may have been afraid of being accused of being a Communist sympathizer, I don't know. But it may have also been one of the things that contributed to the low amount of black participation. Some blacks expressed that I would be fired from my teaching job and would never be able to teach again in California.

As absurd as that may sound, it wasn't too far from being a reality. As a result of my leading our demonstrations, I received a letter from the California State Board of Education informing me to appear at their board meeting to explain to the board why I should not have my teaching license revoked. I called one of our attorneys, David Kroll, and he said he would accompany me to the meeting, which was held in Sacramento, California. We each booked our flight, which we paid for out of our own personal money, took a taxi to the meeting, sat in a room outside their conference room, and waited to be called.

I nervously kept my eyes on the conference room door, wondering if they were really going to try to take my teaching credential away from me. The door opened and they called us into the meeting room. The first thing I saw was a black man seated at the head of the conference table, obviously the chairman. My immediate thought was "oh my God, they're going to have a black man lynch me." The chairman asked me a number of questions to which I answered directly and without emotion. David, my attorney, also responded to some of the chairman's questions. None of their questions seemed particularly tough and threatening. In fact I began to feel that my teaching credential was not in jeopardy and that their committee was trying to scare me into being a "good boy" and stop this civil rights stuff. We were dismissed from the meeting and asked to remain in the waiting room. I sat there along with David and waited for their verdict. Later, the chairman came out, smiling and thanked us for coming. David and I returned to San Diego expecting that I would hear from them later.

I never heard from them again. I was never afraid they would revoke my teaching credential. I was not afraid because I didn't feel they had any legal reason to take away my teaching credential because I felt I was doing a good job as a teacher. That feeling was supported by my being selected as one of the top five beginning teachers in the San Diego Unified School District, and I continued to teach at that level. Maybe I was being naïve, but if they tried I felt I had the support of my school principal, my teacher colleagues, and my students. I'm glad I did not have to put that feeling to a test.

Jail Time

Since I was the chairman and leader of our demonstrations, I was given the larger sentences. I was given a total sentence of 125 days to be spent in the San Diego County Jail. The sentence was to be served on weekends, allowing me to teach school during the week, thereby introducing some magnanimity into this catastrophe. I made the most of my time in jail. I had never seen a jail until I and a few other CORE members were arrested for violating the San Diego Gas & Electric Company injunction during our picketing at their company.

The experience of having a large rolling steel door closed down behind you as you entered the jail, then to be strip-searched before being led to your cell, then having your meals served to you on a tray and slid to you through a slot in the cell door, and finally having to use a toilet that is located openly in the cell for all the cellmates to use, was a very unpleasant experience.

Jail was a scary and lonely place to be, and meant giving up your freedom and your regular life. The first scary part for me was when the officer first took me into the jail. We entered through the rolling steel door. That was a moment when I really felt closed off from the world. My thoughts were that anything could happen to you in here and no one outside would ever know what exactly happened.

I settled in as I was booked, searched, and taken to a holding cell where inmates are held awaiting further action on their case. I was permitted to bring books into the jail until the San Diego County Sheriff petitioned the court with a peremptory writ of prohibition, which was approved and it reversed the decision that allowed me to bring my books into the jail. An annoying part of spending weekends in jail was being subjected to searches every time you entered the jail. That meant removing all your clothes and being searched in every part of your body. However, I looked forward to being released on Sundays to attend church, and being picked up by a wonderful young lady who took me to my apartment where I showered and dressed and went to her apartment where she cooked a nice meal for me and drove me back to jail after church. She would then pick me up from jail when I was released that evening and take me to my apartment where I prepared for teaching school the next day. I have much more to say later about that lady, who became my wife.

Being in jail on weekends was obviously an unpleasant experience, an inconvenience, but I felt a small sacrifice in comparison to what many people around the country were going through, and compared to the potential gains that could be made for blacks and people of color as a result of those sacrifices. An important part of being a civil rights activist for me was having a support group. I don't mean just having the support of the people who joined the marches and attended the meetings, that was important, but having the support of those who love you and really care about you, and understand what you are doing, and why you are doing it, was to me so very important. Those people, in their own way, fed my spirit and gave me strength. I was fortunate to have a loving mother, and the caring of two sisters and four brothers. Although they all lived on the east coast, their love and caring lived inside me. That love and caring also came from a small number of people living in San Diego. The love and caring from family and friends carried me through the jail time, the physical threats, name-calling, the lack of participation and support from many in the black community, and at times, the feeling of being alone. An example of that love and caring was expressed in a letter to Judge Madge Bradley requesting permission for each person signing the letter to serve one day of my jail sentence. The letter appears on the following pages.

Fourteen people signed that petition, men and women, black and white. Their ages ranged from 25 to 58. Although Judge Bradley denied the request, it was a very heartwarming and appreciated gesture.

Leadership Development

After serving my last weekend in jail and fulfilling the two-year probation that I received as part of my sentence, I was mentally exhausted and worn out. I refused to put myself through more of the internal fighting within our CORE chapter. I resigned from CORE and set my sights on something I had wanted to do for a long time—

November 4, 1964

Judge Madge Bradley
San Diego Municipal Court
San Diego, California

Your Honor:

We, the undersigned, respectfully petition to be allowed to serve one day each of the jail sentence imposed on civil rights leader Harold K. Brown. It is our conviction that any legal offense for which he was convicted was committed for the good of humanity and in the spirit of a law that transcends man's local, prevailing statutes. If he is guilty and deserves punishment, we gladly partake of that guilt and sincerely ask to share in that punishment.

Such a petition was granted by Superior Court Judge Vincent Whelan to allow Dr. Charles Collins to serve the sentence imposed on Mrs. Anna Collins. With this precedent in mind, we request that you take whatever legal action is necessary to assign each of us to serve one day in jail in lieu of Harold K. Brown, recognizing that at least one day of the 15 day sentence will be served by Mr. Brown.

	Signature	Address	Age
1.			
2.		2021 Cardinal Dr.	27
3.			
4.	Marie Franklin	4812 Kendall	40
5.		1705 Olean	35
6.	Keith Robinson	3748 Cameo Lane	29
7.	Jane Morgan	806 Manhattan Ct	25
8.	Richard Ulin	7358½ Idaho	25
9.			
10.			
11.		Trophy Dr	
12.			
13.		4464 Shelton	45
14.			

November 4, 1964

Endorsement of Petition

This is to endorse the petition made by the 14 citizens to serve a portion of the jail sentence imposed on civil rights leader Harold K. Brown. It is apparent to us that the actions leading to Mr. Brown's arrest were taken for the good of the whole society and if a price must be paid for Mr. Brown's right to protest against these ancient wrongs, then other members of that society be allowed to help pay that price.

1.	_____	16.	_____
2.	_____	17.	_____
3.	_____	18.	_____
4.	_____	19.	_____
5.	_____	20.	_____
	_____	21.	_____
	_____	22.	_____
	_____	23.	_____
	_____	24.	_____
10.	_____	25.	_____
11.	_____	26.	_____
12.	_____	27.	_____
13.	_____	28.	_____
14.	_____	29.	_____
15.	_____	30.	_____

leadership development combined with economic development. I discussed my ideas with Dr. Charles Collins, my close friend and our public relations chairman. He wrote a grant proposal incorporating my ideas, sent it to the Department of Labor in Washington DC and it was accepted and funded.

The name of the program was "Self Help Through Neighborhood Leadership," and would be sponsored by the San Diego chapter of CORE with me as the executive director. The program was designed to teach leadership skills to 35 residents living in Southeastern San Diego. The skills were to be used to improve the region's neighborhoods. Contained in the program were areas that I considered essential: public speaking (learning Robert's Rules of Order), economics, and community organizing. The program paid a minimum wage to each trainee for a 40-hour week.

The program received funding for one year. I took a leave of absence from teaching school and directed the leadership training program. I was now having as much fun as I had teaching school. I had the trainees' minds focused on the importance of developing black communities through the utilization of economic and political clout. One of the activities I had fun with was when I took the whole group of trainees to the County Voter Registrar's office where we all applied to become registered to sign up voters. When we all walked into the registrar's office, all 35 of us, the Registrar's eyes flew open as wide as a saucer and appeared to be startled and frightened. After he composed himself, he took us through the routine of becoming a registrar and signed all of us up. We returned to our office and each of the trainees selected an area that she/he would sign up people to register to vote. Another example of the trainees' leadership skills was their ability to attend community meetings and use their understanding of Robert's Rules to get things done at those meetings, to present motions and successfully get them passed.

CHAPTER SIX

So Long, San Diego

During the latter part of my year with the leadership program, I was approached by a man I had met previously and he asked me if I was interested in a job with the United States Peace Corps and serving in Africa. He went on to say that there was a deputy director's position in Lesotho, Africa that the Peace Corps was looking to fill.

Because of my great desire to visit the continent of Africa, the land from where we as black people came, the land from where American slaves came, the land of my ancestors—my answer was an immediate yes. I said I would like to hear more about the position at a later time since I was planning to be married and needed to discuss it with my future bride, Lovie LaVerne Webb.

Although my first wife and I had two sons we loved dearly, that marriage ended in divorce: we outgrew each other after ten years. Our children, however, followed my path in sports and although we did not continue to live under the same roof, we spent a lot of time together. I attended most of their basketball games and track meets and helped them develop their basketball skills. I also stressed to them and worked with them to help them set higher educational goals.

In 1965, I met LaVerne shortly after she arrived in San Diego as a result of being recruited from Columbus, Ohio by the

General Dynamics Corporation, to accept the position as a Scientific Computer Systems Developer for the Apollo Space Program. We became good friends and she was very supportive of my involvement in the civil rights movement. After knowing LaVerne for two years, I asked her to marry me. Since we were now planning to get married, I asked her if she would be interested in going to Africa. She responded with an emphatic yes. LaVerne and I were married on June 17, 1967 at Christian Fellowship Church.

At this point in my career I had a desire to investigate opportunities in the business world, and in particular with General Motors Corporation. I decided to start by selling cars part-time at a car dealership in downtown San Diego, Ed Taylor Chevrolet. This gave me the opportunity to work with buyers whose cars were financed by General Motors. I would go to the dealership in the evenings to check on cars for my customers. One evening when I walked into the dealership, another salesman waved to me to come over to the office where he was talking with a customer. LaVerne had just bought a car, but did not know how to drive to General Dynamics. The other salesman introduced me to LaVerne and asked if I would mind showing her the way to drive to General Dynamics. I looked at this beautiful, professionally-dressed, eloquent-looking young lady who was smiling at me and I couldn't get yes out of my mouth fast enough.

Knock! Knock! No Room in the Inn

So, that's how LaVerne and I met. I showed her how to get to General Dynamics, and how to get around San Diego some evenings and on weekends. While looking for housing, LaVerne had called a number of apartments from a list given to her by General Dynamics. Every response to her call asking if there was a vacancy, was that they did not rent to Negroes, when the response was yes, when LaVerne arrived at the apartment she was told that the vacancy had just been filled.

As I showed LaVerne around San Diego, she told me that she was not able to find a place to live because they would not rent to a Negro. Hello again, color monster. I told her I would help her to find an apartment. We spent the day visiting several apartment buildings only to be told they did not rent to Negroes. At the end of the day I remembered a very nice apartment building where I had attended a party given by a white teacher who was a friend and taught with me at the same school. She telephoned the manager of the building and inquired as to whether there was a vacancy. The answer was yes, and he invited her to come see the apartment. I accompanied her to the apartment building. LaVerne rang the doorbell of the apartment manager. The apartment manager opened the door and when LaVerne told him that she was the one who had just called to see the vacant apartment. He told her quickly that the apartment had just been rented after she called. LaVerne asked if she could see the vacant apartment anyhow. He took us through the apartment and LaVerne thought the apartment was very nice and that she would enjoy living there. Well, the manager then said the owner will not rent to Negroes.

I had had enough. I asked the manager to let us talk to the owner. I wanted to talk with the owner and dare him to tell us that he would not rent an apartment to a Negro. The manager then said that the owner lived in Canada and he would try to get in touch with him and then let us know the owner's response. A few days later LaVerne and I called the manager, and he told me that he was not able to reach the owner.

I became angry and told the manager, that if he didn't rent that apartment to this young lady that I would bring 100 Negroes over and we would jump in the pool and take it over until he agreed to rent that apartment to this young lady.

It was no surprise that he then agreed he would rent the apartment to her.

I feel that sometimes you have to confront the color monster head on with militant and direct action to break the chain of racial injustice. The color monster remains strong because of the fear to attack it.

That fear was alive and well in San Diego's black community, demonstrated by the wife of a well-known black minister. Before LaVerne left Ohio she was given the name of a prominent black minister in San Diego who was a friend of her minister. The minister's wife offered to help LaVerne find an apartment and drove her around to different apartment buildings on the list provided to LaVerne by General Dynamics, the company that recruited her to San Diego. The minister's wife would drive LaVerne to each apartment building but would pass the apartment building and park a block or two away and wait while LaVerne would walk back to the apartment. The minister's wife explained to LaVerne that she didn't want anybody to know she was doing this because "they" might think her husband was behind this and she was fearful that if "they" thought her husband was involved with this, it would be harmful to her husband.

It was very nice of the minister's wife to help LaVerne find an apartment, even though it was not successful, she tried to help. But I wonder what kind of harm she thought would come to her husband if "they" found out that she was helping LaVerne look for an apartment. Obviously it was because the minister's wife was taking LaVerne to areas outside Southeast San Diego, the area where blacks were confined to live. When LaVerne told me what the minister's wife told her, I felt so sorry for the minister's wife and for her husband. They and many more black people lived in fear of "they."

LaVerne and I got to know each other better and months later we were dating and enjoyed each other. She had moved into her apartment, owned a car, and was driving to General Dynamics. One day when we were in her car going to a restaurant, she had the radio on and the voice on the radio announced that the CORE demonstrators against the Bank of America were receiving sentences today. The announcer went on to say that Hal Brown, the chairman of CORE, and several others were given jail sentences. Since I saw no reaction from LaVerne, I asked her if she heard what the announcer said. She said yes. I asked if she knew that he was talking about me. She nonchalantly said yes.

I couldn't believe her reaction. I thought if she heard that, it would be the last time she would go on a date with me. That is why I never mentioned that I was active in the civil rights movement and the chairman of CORE. I was accustomed to having many black professionals in San Diego treat me as a pariah, like I had some contagious disease that they should not be around. So I was afraid that LaVerne was one of those middle-class Negroes who didn't want anything to do with those civil rights people.

Boy, was I wrong about LaVerne. Her nonchalance to the radio announcement surprised me. I later learned why she was not surprised or in the least disturbed when she heard the radio announcement. LaVerne was born and grew up in Alabama. Her father was a Baptist minister and her mother was an elementary school teacher. After her brothers left home, her father, taught his daughters how to shoot a gun for protection in fear of what whites might do to harm him and their family at any time if they did not like something that he did or said, or something that they thought he did or said. This was one of many things that blacks lived with growing up in the South.

LaVerne was a student at Alabama State University when the lunch counter protest demonstrations took place at A&T University in North Carolina, and when the students at her university, joined the protest by holding a lunch counter sit-in in Montgomery, she joined the protest. She knew Dr. Martin Luther King Jr. and occasionally attended his church, and participated in the Montgomery bus boycott. Dr. King was an occasional visitor and speaker at her university. She was exposed to many instances of cruelty by whites in the south toward their Negro citizens.

She was exposed to the many indignities that blacks suffer when they came in contact with whites: forced to drink water out of a separate fountain, if there was one; forced to use a separate bathroom, if there was one; forced to sit upstairs at a movie theater away from whites; not being able to try on clothes at a clothing store; being forced to address all white people, including children, as Mr. and Mrs., while blacks are being addressed as boy or girl regardless of their age; being forced to step off the sidewalk and let a white person pass; forced as a paid passenger to ride in the back of the bus or in a separate part of the train; and, of course, not allowed to vote.

So, LaVerne saw a lot and experienced a lot long before she met me. That explains why she didn't react the way I expected her to react when she heard the announcement on her car radio that the fellow she recently met and was sitting next to her was the person the announcer said was going to jail. We began to see each other regularly and liked being together.

Shortly after LaVerne and I began dating, I received notice from the Municipal Court that I was to begin serving my sentence. When that time arrived, LaVerne drove me to the jail, as she did each weekend until I had served all my time. She later told me that each time when the steel door rolled down behind me and she heard the door slam shut, she would begin praying for my safety. We began to look forward to seeing each other every evening and soon I knew I was falling in love. One day while sitting in her apartment I told her that I felt we would make a terrific team. After two years of dating I asked her to marry me, and she said yes.

At our wedding, LaVerne was joined by some of her family from the East Coast and I was joined by my close friend Dr. Ernest Hartzog, who grew up in the same town as I did, York Pennsylvania, where we were friends and teammates. Ernie was my Best Man at our wedding.

Although I was very reluctant to give up my position as executive director of the leadership program to travel to Africa, I felt I could not turn down this opportunity. I thought I could turn over the program to some capable person and I could join the program again in some capacity when I returned to the United States. I had further discussions with the person representing the Peace Corps, completed an application, was invited to Washington DC for a series of interviews, and was hired as the deputy director of the United States Peace Corps in Lesotho, Africa.

As I said my goodbyes to the leadership trainees and friends, I was honored with a Harold Brown Day as a farewell from the city of San Diego. The Harold Brown Day began with a picnic sponsored by the leadership trainees and held at Mountain View Park in Southeast San Diego. We were having great fun and I was enjoying the send-off when an incident happened that could have caused me my life.

A fellow showed up at the picnic and proceeded to give one of our lady trainees, who was serving food, a hard time. I intervened, telling him to give her a break. He turned to me, mad as hell. He yelled obscenities and ran to his car and came back running toward me with a knife in his hand, shouting at me.

My oldest son, Michael, who was eight years old, grabbed an empty glass Coke bottle and said "here, Dad." I took the bottle but before the fellow could get to me, a female friend of mine stepped in front of me and was reaching under her clothes at the top chest. Before she brought out whatever she was carrying, a friend of the fellow who was running toward me with a knife, grabbed him with both arms and lifted him and held him to keep him from getting to me.

The fellow who stopped his friend with the knife yelled to me "man, he will kill you he just got out of prison for killing somebody."

I was very upset, but I was also angry and wished I had something to put that fellow out of his misery. While I adopted the strategy of non-e violence as the tool to be used to fight against racism, I was not a pacifist, and this was not a civil rights demonstration. I was very lucky that I had a friend who put her life in jeopardy to save mine. I was also lucky that the fellow had a friend at the picnic who didn't want to see his friend go back to prison.

I left the picnic with my two sons, Michael and Stephen, and my fiancée and went home. Harold Brown Day then ended with a wonderful dinner at one of the downtown hotels which was attended by a large number of people from the city of San Diego. I was joined at the dinner by my new bride and my two sons. It was a lovely occasion.

So a few weeks after our marriage, LaVerne and I moved to Washington DC, where we went through orientation and language training in the Basotho language for the trip. Soon after our language training we were off to Lesotho, Africa, a country located in the southern part of Africa and completely surrounded by South Africa, the land of apartheid.

Me and My Wife, LaVerne

CHAPTER SEVEN

Hello, Africa

We had a day-long layover in Johannesburg before continuing on a flight the next day to Lesotho. This was in 1967, when apartheid was at its height. Apartheid was a system of institutionalized racial segregation and discrimination that existed in South Africa. It was based on white supremacy using the color of one's skin—black, colored, and Indian—for the repression of the African and Indian majority of the population for the benefit of whites.

When we landed in Johannesburg, LaVerne and I were approached by airport officials, who asked for our passports, and told us to follow them. We followed them and were led to the upper floor of the airport and taken to a room where we were to spend the night. We were not allowed to leave the room until our flight to Lesotho was ready the following day. It became obvious to me at that time that our passports had been confiscated and we were confined to this room in the airport. In other words, we were in jail, even if the room we were confined to was not called a jail.

The next morning when we awoke I decided that I would test this apartheid mess and take a stroll outside the airport where my wife and I were not allowed to go. I didn't tell LaVerne what I was going to do because I knew she would be afraid for me and would try to talk me out of it. I left the inside of the airport terminal and proceeded to walk outside. I then heard my name being called over the public address system to report to the gate.

I ignored the call. I saw two white men come and stand close to me while looking in another direction. I heard them talking in a low voice, but not looking at me. I eventually realized they were talking to me and asking if everything was okay. I muttered something like "I guess so," and they disappeared. I figured they must have been from the American Embassy because they were white and spoke like Americans, and they may have been concerned about me because of my Peace Corps position as an official representative of the United States government.

I later learned that it was the policy of the South African government to hold a room or rooms upstairs at the airport for African government officials traveling from other African countries and other black dignitaries who must stay overnight for a flight the next day. I found it more than interesting that the South African government, which was governed by all whites and is a minority of the country's population of black people, was able to rule that country by discriminating and segregating all nonwhite people and restricting them to low or no jobs, segregated poor housing, and few educational opportunities. Sound familiar? South Africa and the U.S. had very similar political and socioeconomic systems, both based on color: one called apartheid, the other, racism.

Although I knew about apartheid and of course was very familiar with racism, it seemed to me that the unfairness of it all was too much to ask people to endure. At times I felt the hopelessness to be overwhelming. However, I kept believing that our day would come. My passion to be in Africa was very strong and propelled me to journey on.

I eventually met up with LaVerne inside the airport and we were escorted to the gate for our flight. Our passports were returned to us and we boarded a small plane that would take us a short distance to a small landing field in Maseru, the capital city of Lesotho. LaVerne and I and a few other passengers were the only passengers on the plane.

When we landed and stepped outside the plane, the feeling I had was so emotionally charged with happiness and elation that I literally kneeled and kissed the ground. I could not believe that I was finally standing on the land of our ancestors and would have the opportunity to live here for a while. We were met by our Peace Corps Director, Dave Sherwood, who had made arrangements for us to stay at the hotel in Maseru while our home was being built. When I saw Dave, my first thought was to ask him why he didn't tell us about the situation at the Johannesburg airport. However, I ended up not mentioning it. Dave was white and an American, and I felt it would embarrass him to talk about it. But I also wondered why we were not informed of the airport situation during our orientation in Washington DC.

After I gathered my emotions about being in Africa, LaVerne and I got our luggage, put it into Dave's Land Rover, and Dave drove us to Lancers Inn where, as I said, we would be staying until our home was completed. Dave dropped us off and said he would see me tomorrow at the Peace Corps office. The Peace Corps office was within walking distance of Lancers Inn.

Dave Sherwood, Peace Corps Director and me waiting for volunteers to arrive

We walked into Lancers Inn and checked in. We were taken to one of the rooms where we would live until our home was completed. The room accommodations were satisfactory enough, and we were anxious to get to know Maseru, the capital of Lesotho.

But we soon found out that the room where we were staying was a room strictly for African and other black guests. Although LaVerne and I aren't Africans, the color of our skin determined our status, and again, the highest status is given to those with white skin, and all others are given a low status, even in an African country.

Here's this color thing again. It really hurt me to see that white people were in control of a black country. Yes, Lesotho had an African Prime Minister, an African King, and African political parties, but Lesotho was under the control of white South Africa. The saving grace for me—what saved my sanity—was the Basotho people. They were kind, loving people who accepted us as one of them. They showed us so much love, kindness, and friendship. They even looked like us, or rather, we looked like them.

LaVerne and I became friends with many of them and were guests in their homes. LaVerne and I only spoke a little of the Basotho language, Sesotho, but I had the greetings down pat, so much so that those who did not know me thought I was one of them, a Mosotho. I would later tell them that I was an American, which many times started a long conversation. The Basotho spoke English as well as their own language, so communication was easy. Although Laverne and I fell in love with the Basotho people and were treated so well by them, I still could not forget the black/white curse that seemed to follow me throughout my life. Here I am in Africa, the land of my ancestry, the world I was dying to see, and I found confirmation of the propaganda taught in America: that white is good and powerful and black is bad and powerless.

Lesotho is a country the size of the state Maryland and had a population of approximately one million at the time. It was formerly a British protectorate and became an independent country in 1966. It would be described as a poor country by American standards. It had some farming, but most of the land was eroded and mountainous and most of the men worked in the mines of South Africa and were away from home most of the year. The few businesses that existed in Lesotho were owned by white South Africans.

We ate our meals at Lancers Inn, and I sometimes ate with friends at the Maseru Café, which was also close to where we lived. After LaVerne and I unpacked our clothes and settled in, we walked to the Peace Corps office and met the other staff members. There were three staff members and Dave the director who arrived a few weeks before we did to set up the office. The fourth staff person, a medical doctor and his wife, arrived a few weeks later. All the staff members other than me were white. The United States also had a Charge d'Affaires office located in Lesotho. That staff was also white.

The Peace Corps provided Land Rover vehicles for us, so after the introductions I set up my office and LaVerne and I drove back to Lancers Inn. The next day I returned to the office to begin my first full day on the job. Dave and I and the other staff members began to plan for the arrival of the 70 Peace Corps volunteers who were to arrive in a couple months. A couple of months passed and LaVerne and I had moved into our house. The house, I was informed, was owned by a Mosotho and was being rented by the Peace Corps. The house was much too large for the two of us but we used it to entertain Mosotho guests and Peace Corps volunteers.

The time had now arrived to go to the airport and welcome the arrival of the Peace Corps volunteers. The plane arrived and Dave and I, along with LaVerne and the other staff members, were excited to meet the volunteers. As the volunteers deplaned one by one it hit me that all these volunteers are white. I was aware that one of Lesotho's political parties, and its leader, were strongly opposed to having the Peace Corps in Lesotho and had accused the Peace Corps of being the CIA and coming to spy on the Basotho. That made no sense to me, because what did Lesotho have that the United States wanted to spy on? But many in Lesotho were well aware of the Vietnam War and viewed the United States as the enemy of people of color.

So when I saw all the volunteers pouring out of the plane and all were white except three, I said to myself, "Oh! Oh! I don't think this is going to be good." However, I kept my thoughts to myself and hoped for the best. I was glad to see the volunteers and I looked forward to working with them. As the Deputy Director of the Peace Corps in Lesotho, my job was to oversee the education part of the Peace Corps program and to supervise the 30 volunteers who were assigned to teach in the schools throughout the 10 Lesotho districts. The others were assigned to the areas of public health and community development.

After meeting and chatting with all the volunteers, they each were taken to their respective districts where they met with their school principals, while the other volunteers were taken to their assignments. Shortly after all the volunteers were settled in, the Prime Minister of Lesotho held a welcoming party for the Peace

Corps. There was lots of wonderful music and dancing, with the Prime Minister delighting us with his solo performance of the boot dance. However, the party ended, and after the volunteers, the staff and I began to go on with our work, we learned through the Maseru newspaper that many of the Basotho people were very unhappy about the Peace Corps being in Lesotho.

The leader of the Opposition Party, Mr. Ntsu Mokhehle, held large gatherings where he denounced the Peace Corps as spies and supporters of South Africa's apartheid. There seemed to be a large number of Basotho who agreed with him based on those large gatherings, and what I heard from talking with different people who I met. The more I talked with the Basotho people, the more I felt that there was strong anti-American feeling. They resented America's killing of the Vietnamese people during the war, and they were aware of America's treatment of the American Negro. Mr. Mokhehle, I was told by some of the people who visited us at our home, had won the election as Lesotho's Prime Minister but was denied the office by the intervention of South Africa, who supported the other candidate for the presidency, Mr. Leabua Jonathan, who expressed no opposition to South Africa's system of apartheid.

Mr. Jonathan as the Prime Minister, then placed the King of Lesotho, King Moshoeshoe, under house arrest because of his opposition to South Africa's apartheid. The King was under house arrest when we arrived in Lesotho. I was not aware of this strong feeling that many Basotho had against the Peace Corps, nor was I aware of their resentment toward Americans. My orientation into the Peace Corps did not include that kind of information. Weeks and months passed while I had to live with the realization that I, as a civil rights activists, who had spent years fighting against racism in America, was now in a position where I am involved in supporting a government that supports racism in South Africa, and being resented by the Lesotho people who I have become to love. I didn't come to Africa to fight racism in South Africa, but I didn't come to support it either.

Although I was not confronted by any of the Basotho people, my wife was, and that made me very angry. I went looking for the man who verbally attacked LaVerne so I could confront him, but I couldn't find him. We were told that LaVerne was even verbally attacked at some of the political meetings. Interestingly, no one ever attacked or criticized me personally. I wondered why.

As time went by, the Basotho people learned more about LaVerne and me, where we lived in America, our families, and how it was to be a Negro living in America. As they got to know us they — chiefs, teachers, and others we got to know—became frequent visitors to our home. They would just drop by. They would talk about their lives as Africans, where they were born and grew up, and about Lesotho and South Africa. Some lived in South Africa and moved to Lesotho to escape apartheid. Others left South Africa because they were Freedom Fighters and had to leave the country. I shared with them the conditions under which we as Negroes lived in America. I shared with them my role in the civil rights movement as the chairman of San Diego CORE. In Lesotho, women did not sit with men while talking and drinking alcoholic beverages, so LaVerne did not participate with us in the discussion when a group of men

Me visiting a Lesotho Village

came to our home. But we had a number of occasions when LaVerne and I would often be invited by others to visit and have dinner and discussions at their homes. It was such a pleasure and so enjoyable when LaVerne and I would be invited by a couple to dinner. The Basotho were always so, what we call it in America, low-key. What I call it is calm, quiet, and peaceful.

Being in Lesotho was great fun in spite of the political situation. LaVerne set up a library in one of the hospitals and tutored some young people in mathematics. LaVerne was a mathematics teacher early in her professional career and then became a mathematician for North American Aviation and later a computer systems engineer with IBM Corporation. Her minor in college was in library science, so when she was not traveling with me visiting Peace Corp volunteers, she was busy enjoying tutoring young students in mathematics and setting up the library. It should be noted that Lesotho has one of the highest literacy rates in Africa. According to recent estimates, 85 percent of those older than 14 are literate.

I found that the Basotho population consisted of very sophisticated and informed people. I enjoyed my conversations with them at our home, at their homes, at Lancers Inn, or having a drink at some of the districts outside Maseru when I was visiting the volunteers. Their understanding of what was going on around the world impressed me very much and made me wish that my fellow Americans were as aware and interested in the affairs of the world as the Basotho who lived in a small country with no sophisticated educational system. A large percentage of the population was living on meager incomes and probably never traveled outside of the district where they lived. There was little opportunity for the Basotho to develop their country economically while living under the control of the South African government.

My heart ached for them as I compared my standard of living with so many of the Basotho who worked for two dollars a day. LaVerne and I felt guilty to hire a housekeeper and gardener and pay them two dollars a day, so we tried to pay them much more but were criticized by those who hired help and did not want to pay higher wages. We were accused of upsetting the current system of employee wages. So, we had to limit our pay to slightly more than the going wages.

As an African American and civil rights activist and dealing with our own apartheid in America, it was becoming increasingly more difficult for me to justify being in Lesotho and being a part of the support of apartheid as a representative of the American government, which quietly accepted the South African government's control of Lesotho as well as South Africa's system of apartheid. America at the time had companies doing business in South Africa and those companies were being quiet about the apartheid system. As I mentioned earlier, I had no intentions nor did I have any desire to address the issue of South African apartheid and Lesotho's victimization of apartheid. But the longer I remained in Lesotho, and the more I heard stories from the Basotho who previously lived in South Africa, and from some who were South African freedom fighters, now refugees in Lesotho, the more difficult it was for me to justify my being in Lesotho as the deputy director of the Peace Corps. LaVerne and I listened to many stories told to us by the Basotho that expressed the cruelty and inhumane treatment heaped on Africans by South African whites. Black South Africans had to carry passes to identify themselves, were restricted to live in specific areas separate from whites, only given the lowest jobs or no jobs, have much less opportunities for education, were stopped and arrested for trumped up charges, put in jail, and placed in the hands of white farmers who use them to work on their farms for no pay - a modified form of slavery.

When arrested, since the police could not or would not pronounce or spell their names, the arrestees were given names like bicycle and other demeaning names. These stories reminded me of the days when I was growing up being called nigger, sambo, and chocolate drop, among others. These names were meant to demean and embarrass me, and reinforce the power and superiority of whites. This same method was used by white South Africans against black South Africans. These stories told to me and LaVerne also triggered memories in her since she was born and grew up in Alabama, and is quite aware of how blacks were treated in the South. As the months passed and our relationship with the Basotho people strengthened, I was invited to speak at the high school in Maseru and at the University of Lesotho, Botswana and Swaziland, which was located just outside Maseru. The high school students, dressed in their school uniforms, were full of questions about America and of course the life of Negroes in America. It was delightful to see such courteous boys and girls eager for an education.

My speech at the University was just as delightful, but even more enjoyable. As I mentioned, this was the University of Lesotho, Botswana and Swaziland. Students attending the University were from those three countries. What amazed me, I was told that many of the students who did not have transportation to get to the university had to walk many miles through mountainous rough conditions just to get to the university. The students were delighted to see an American Negro and had many questions. I thoroughly enjoyed the time I spent with them. I should take a moment to explain that I was not in Lesotho to throw barbs at the United States or to embarrass the U.S. for its treatment of us blacks, and I did not do so, nor did I have any desire to. However, neither was I in Lesotho to lie or apologize for that treatment.

Lesotho's high schools where I visited

When asked questions about the Negro in America, I answered them truthfully, telling about the wonderful things America has to offer, but many of those things were not available to Blacks. Besides, the Basotho people are an informed people who may not have ever seen an American Negro, but they knew about the American Negro, as illustrated by the following story.

LaVerne and I were traveling to one of the outlying districts where we met a group of Basotho sitting around a rondoval (hut) chatting. As we approached the group, one elderly lady came up to greet us. She said hello in her Sesotho language and we responded in Sesotho. The woman looked at us kind of quizzically, and said to us in her language where do you live or where are you from. We replied, America.

She looked astounded and somewhat sad, and said to us in English, "wow!" Then she said with sadness in her eyes, "Are you free? Why you don't come back home?"

She was asking if we were free from slavery. I can't remember much after that as I fought to hold back my tears. She asked that question as though she was well aware that LaVerne and I were two of those Negroes who were captured and sold into slavery in America and were badly mistreated. The way she said it sounded like she believed that LaVerne and I had only been gone from our home in Africa for a few years.

The connection between LaVerne and me and the Bosotho people was strong and growing stronger. While I was enjoying my job in the Peace Corp and working with volunteers, I was becoming more aware of the political situation in Lesotho. I learned much about the history of Lesotho and its current political problems. Mr. Mohekle and his political party continued to attack the Peace Corps's presence in Lesotho, and the Vietnam War raged on. All the while the king is under house arrest. It was now known that I had spoken at the high school and the University, which in no way was secret or meant to be. I felt I was just doing my job by getting to know the Basotho and socializing with them whenever possible.

One of my responsibilities as the deputy director was to write reports of my activities and experiences, and to send those reports to the Director of the US Peace Corps in Washington DC. This I gladly did, and proudly shared my findings of the situation in Lesotho and offered my recommendation when I felt it appropriate. One of my recommendations was that I felt we would be helping the Basotho

*LaVerne and King Moshoeshoe's
staff members*

*Peace Corps Official From Washington, D.C.,
our gardener and his wife at our home*

Lesotho Family whose home we visited

*Peace Corps volunteer and high school
students at our home*

more if we educated them to be teachers in their schools, rather than having our volunteers teaching in their schools, and taking the jobs that the Basotho would have. Another recommendation I made was to recruit volunteers who were experienced with skills in technical areas and mix them with volunteers right out of college. It is my understanding that this is now being done in the Peace Corps. In my reports I also made one prediction. I predicted that Mr. Mohehle and his party would win the next Prime Minister election and we should be prepared for that. Although LaVerne and I had left Lesotho by the time of the next election, I understand Prime Minister Leabua Jonathan lost his position as prime minister to Mr. Ntsu Mohekle. My reports were typed by our Peace Corps secretary and forwarded to Washington DC.

I later began to hear that the South African government was unhappy with my speaking at the high school and the University, and also for entertaining Basotho in our home. I was accused in the Johannesburg newspaper of "trying to bring black power to Africa." I couldn't help but see what the words of that accusation revealed. It's interesting to note that I was never approached by the US Charge d'Affaires's or anyone from his office expressing any concern about my speeches or involvement with the Basotho people, nor did our Peace Corps director ever express any concern with any of my activities. In fact I had no relationship with anyone at the Charge d'Affaires' office except for playing tennis with them once or twice.

As I look back I can see that things were heating up as far as my stay in Lesotho was concerned. I found it interesting that I, as the Peace Corps Deputy Director, never met Prime Minister Jonathan

LaVerne and me visiting with King Moshoeshoe

or was I ever invited to any of his events. However, King Mosheswe, who was under house arrest, invited LaVerne and me to a party at his palace, which we enjoyed very much. LaVerne had several dances with the King and I danced with the Queen. I suspect that the reason I never met Prime Minister Jonathan, nor was ever invited to any of his social affairs, was that members of the Lesotho Peace Corps were not allowed to enter South Africa, therefore I probably didn't make it onto his invitation list.

Also, my being black could have been another reason. I found it very interesting, but not surprising, that South Africa would not allow anyone associated with the Lesotho Peace Corps to enter its country. However, I was disappointed that the American government agreed to it. Time passed, the Vietnam War was still in the news and the fight for freedom in the U.S. was going hot and heavy. Demonstrations and marches against racial injustices were held around the country. Again, interestingly, the turmoil at home in the U.S. was never mentioned or discussed with me and LaVerne by anyone in the Peace Corps or the Charge d'Affaires' staff. It should be clear that I draw no conclusions as to why the Americans in Lesotho never mentioned the race issue to me. It should also be clear that nothing was ever said to me about my speaking at the high school or my socializing with the Basotho people. I never thought about not having discussed the racial issue or apartheid with my fellow Americans. I guess I thought if they wanted to talk with me and LaVerne about it, they would bring up the issue. I was well aware that it was extremely difficult for most white Americans to discuss the issue of race in America.

CHAPTER EIGHT

Dr. Martin Luther King Jr.'s Assassination

More months passed. The only time I recall receiving any communication from the Charge d'Affaires' office was when LaVerne and I heard the devastating news that Dr. Martin Luther King Jr. had been shot and killed.

It was the most horrifying and the most hurtful news I had ever received in my life. LaVerne and I cried until there were no more tears. I cursed until there were no more words. Killing Martin Luther King, the most recognized symbol of the civil rights movement, was an attempt to kill the civil rights movement and put blacks back to the "Mr. Charlie" and "Boss Man" days, when whites treated blacks of any age as children, and white superiority was commonly practiced throughout the nation. Killing the civil rights movement would mean that the country would not have to tolerate blacks protesting against racial discrimination, segregation, and unjust treatment of black citizens—so they thought.

After the tears came anger: lots of it. I told LaVerne to start thinking about leaving Lesotho because we were needed at home to do what we could to continue our struggle for equality and freedom.

But we were 10,000 miles away and would not be able to participate in a memorial service to celebrate Dr. King's life. So, I thought, "Let's have a memorial service here in Lesotho." LaVerne agreed.

I went to the African Methodist Episcopal Church in Maseru and explained to the minister that we would like to hold a memorial service for Dr. King at his church. The minister said he would be happy to have the memorial service held at his church and he would organize the service. He asked me to give the eulogy and asked LaVerne if she would sing a hymn. It was almost as though he knew LaVerne had a beautiful voice and sang in a choir back home, which both were true.

We both said yes and began the slow process of healing after hearing the news of Dr. King's death. LaVerne began to practice the hymn she decided to sing, and I started writing the eulogy. Time passed slowly, but the day of the memorial service arrived. LaVerne and I arrived at the church early to meet with the minister, who explained how the service would be conducted and showed us our seats in the pulpit. He then introduced us to the man who would also be a speaker, and to the man who would be my interpreter. People began to arrive at the church and quietly took their seats. LaVerne and I had no idea of how many people would attend. We took our seats and watched the church gradually fill to capacity. We had no idea of how the people found out about the service, but they were there.

The program started and before I was introduced to give the eulogy, we were all astounded when the King of Lesotho entered the church and took a seat at the front. My eyeballs popped out of my head. I couldn't believe that King Moshoeshoe, who was under house arrest by the Lesotho government, was attending the memorial service for Dr. King. My heart was swelling with pride and thankfulness.

LaVerne was then introduced and beautifully sang "Steal Away," a Negro Spiritual, and received a thunderous applause. I was then introduced, along with my interpreter, and delivered these words to the attendees. I wanted to share with the attendees who Dr. King was and what he meant to black Americans and to the United States of America. My eulogy appears below.

EULOGY

The best words to describe the assassination of Dr. Martin Luther King, Jr. are those that I received from a friend yesterday. The words are that he was such a good man and because of that, the good in man came out in all its glory. He was such a good man, and because of that, the evil in man came out in all its fury.

Dr. Martin Luther King Jr., a man born with black skin in a nation where that was looked upon as being less than a full citizen. Dr. King was born in Atlanta, Georgia in 1929. Georgia is a state known for its oppression of black Americans. Georgia is a southern state in America in the same category as Mississippi, Alabama, Louisiana, and Tennessee. Martin Luther King grew up under the racism of the white majority. It was inevitable that he should want to correct the injustices suffered by his black brothers and sisters in America.

As he grew up in Atlanta, he finished high school and attended Morehouse University. After graduation, he went on to receive his PhD from Boston University.

Dr. King began on his road to international fame when he challenged the white segregation of Montgomery Alabama, where blacks, among other things, had to ride in the back of the bus provided for public transportation, reserving other seats up front for whites. Dr. King and his followers organized the black citizens of Montgomery and boycotted the bus company. This financially hurt the owners of the bus company so badly that the segregation of black and white passengers was wiped away.

The black man's struggle for freedom was now in motion again, and Dr. King took his fight to other American cities, challenging segregation and discrimination in all areas of American life. The movement grew and so did Dr. King, as his name became the symbol of the black man's struggle for freedom in America.

Dr. King was a philosopher. He adopted the philosophy of nonviolence to obtain the freedom he so eloquently articulated. He preached peace and love to all who listened and unfortunately some did not listen and some of those who listened did not act. Dr. King preached nonviolence to his Afro-American people in spite of the hatred and brutality directed at them.

And we followed him. We suffered with him. We were spat on, kicked, beaten, hosed down with powerful forces of water, prodded by police using electric prods, put in jail and murdered. We, as Afro-Americans, suffered with Dr. King the atrocities of white oppression. He was our leader, the symbol of our struggle. He embraced the philosophy of nonviolence.

Dr. King was an orator. He grew up under a father who was a Baptist minister. Dr. King himself became a Baptist minister at Dexter Avenue Baptist Church in Montgomery, Alabama. Dr. King's speeches on civil rights were just as potent as his Sunday sermons. They reached way down to the soul of every black American and made them share his dream that one day the American black man would break all the chains of slavery and would one day completely be free.

Dr. King took his message to every corner of America to both black and whites. He inspired not only the black Americans but some of the whites as well. Some whites began to take an active part in the civil rights movement.

Dr. King was a husband and a father. He was survived by his wife and four children. His wife also took an active part in the struggle along with her husband. She often joined him on marches and she would use her singing talent to raise money to support the struggle by giving concerts throughout America.

Dr. King was an author. He took time out of his busy schedule to write the books entitled Stride Toward Freedom: The Montgomery Story; Why We Can't Wait; and Where Do We Go From Here: Chaos or Community?

Dr. King was a man of men. He chose to fight for those things that are "just" according to God. Dr. King was America's conscience. Dr. King IS America's conscience. Dr. King is the conscience of mankind and we will never let mankind forget. Dr. King is the sanity of America and that sanity must not die with Dr. King.

There is no turning back. The black man's struggle against white domination will continue until we are completely free. Dr. King led us down the road of nonviolence *to achieve this goal. Will his absence on earth cause us to take another course?*

So, we say goodbye to this great man. He has left the struggle now, gone to join Malcolm X, Medger Evers and the countless numbers of black Americans who perished from the earth at the hands of white racism. Rest in peace my brother.

I felt that the eulogy was well received and appreciated, as was LaVerne's hymn. The program ended and LaVerne and I could not thank the minister enough for organizing this service and for the use of his church.

Although I hated to leave Lesotho, I was determined and anxious to return to the U.S. LaVerne was not happy at all about leaving Lesotho, but understood my feelings about wanting to get back home and continue working for the progress of black America. I notified Dave Sherwood, our Peace Corps Director, that we were leaving Lesotho. He informed the national Peace Corps office who made the travel plans for our return to the U.S. In the remaining days of our stay in Lesotho we said our goodbyes, packed our belongings, and shipped them to Washington DC.

When we arrived at the airport on our day of departure, we noticed that there were an unusual number of people standing around. We soon learned that the people came to the airport to say goodbye to us. They were wearing their Basotho blankets, some in suits, and others in casual dress. It was obvious that many had walked a long distance to reach the airport. We had no idea that we would receive a send off from the Basotho people. They brought gifts: Basotho blankets, a Basotho hat, a cane, beads, and a cassette tape of a conversation we had with one of our friends who visited us in our home.

LaVerne and I were in tears as we shook hands with all of those who came to say goodbye. In that moment, I could not get the village woman's words out of my head: "Why you not come back home?"

"You go there," she said, "they kill you." I was hoping she didn't know something that I did not.

LaVerne and I boarded the plane carrying our gifts, and took our seats when I received another surprise. A white lady approached me and said she was a reporter with the Johannesburg newspaper, and she would like to interview me before the plane departed; I agreed. She asked me a number of questions about why I chose to return to the U.S. and asked my opinions about apartheid and the race issue in America. I have no idea as to whether the interview appeared in the newspaper, but I was happy to share my feelings about apartheid and racism in the U.S. with the South African news reporter. LaVerne and I sat back in our seats and waved to the people who came to the airport to say goodbye to us.

Visiting Zambia, Tanzania and Kenya

Now, we were on our way back to the U.S., but we had decided that we would visit other African countries on our way back home. We planned to visit Lusaka, the capital of Zambia; Dar es

Salaam, Tanzania; and Nairobi, Kenya. During the last days of our time in Lesotho, a friend gave us the name of a person who was an official in the government of Zambia and this person contacted us at the hotel where we were staying, and welcomed us to Zambia. The next day we were told we had a visitor. The visitor greeted us very warmly and told us that we should not be staying in a hotel and that he had arranged for us to live with a family there in Lusaka. He then took us to the home to meet the family where we would be staying. The family was from Jamaica and the man worked in the Zambian government. LaVerne and I were more than pleased that we were being so well received. We were taken back to the hotel where we packed our clothes, checked out of the hotel, and were driven back to the home where we would be staying during our time in Zambia. We experienced many pleasant moments with our host family, including getting to know them and sharing our life stories.

We devoted a lot of time discussing the future development of Zambia and African Americans in the United States. Through our discussions, we decided that there should be a program similar to the U.S. Peace Corps, whose purpose would be to bring black Americans with professional skills to Zambia to work with the Zambian government. We agreed that if he would write the proposal, I would work on trying to get such a program started in the U.S. Unfortunately, I was unable to generate any interest in America in forming such a program. Remember, the year was 1968, when protest demonstrations and other civic unrest were occupying the attention of most people. Also, the feeling of most African-Americans, with few exceptions, was that Africa was a far distant country (not a continent) and a place that was poor and undeveloped, and a place they were not interested in visiting. I suppose much of that perception was the result of seeing Tarzan movies, which had a white man scantily dressed, cast in the role of Tarzan— – King of the jungle. The movie showed Africans, also scantily dressed in "jungle" attire carrying spears, and showing great fear of Tarzan, the king of the jungle.

While in Zambia, LaVerne and I got to see a lot of Lusaka and were able to visit with other Zambians through the introductions of our host. One memorable event was being invited to a welcoming back home reception for President Kenneth Kaunda, who was the president of Zambia at that time. The reception was held at the airport in Lusaka and LaVerne and I were happy and honored to be invited to be a part of the group that was welcoming President Kaunda back from his trip.

I must insert here that being in Africa had a tremendous impact on my life. Growing up in America, in York, Pennsylvania, and as an adult in San Diego, California, I never had the experience of seeing a black person who was part of the leadership of the city, county, state, or country. The only leadership I saw was white men.

Now, through my experience in Africa, I have met the king of a country and a president of a different country. The very serious problem I had with being an American and growing up and living in America, was that I didn't see people who looked like me, had skin color like mine, and who were among the leadership of the cities, counties, states, and countries. I believe the brain recognized this, stored it, and when it saw someone that is inconsistent with what was stored there, the brain recognizes this and reacts in some way.

Well, my brain reacted: and I said to myself, WOW! No wonder I never felt that America was really my country. It was their country and I was merely living in it at the pleasure of those who didn't look like me. Watching people who looked like me, kneeling, and bowing to honor their leader, who also looked like me, was a sobering and exciting experience for me and my brain. I believe that many Americans had the same experience and that even today, 50 years after we returned home from Africa, many black Americans still have problems with following, respecting, and honoring the leadership of a black person. I hope I'm wrong.

The time came for us to leave Zambia and head for Tanzania. The man who hosted our stay in Zambia told us that he had notified a person in Dar es Salaam that we were coming to visit Tanzania, and he would like for him to host us while we were there. When we arrived in Dar es Salaam, sure enough, there were several men who were at the airport to meet us and take us to our hotel. Again, LaVerne and I were overwhelmed with the friendship and brotherly treatment that we received.

Our stay in Tanzania was a very pleasant and memorable one. As in Lesotho and Zambia, we exchanged stories about ourselves, were introduced to others, and had great fun. The men who met us at the airport informed us that they were freedom fighters from South Africa and now live in Tanzania. I found it interesting and most revealing that in America the freedom fighters of South Africa were described as terrorists, not freedom fighters. After exchanging lots of stories about their struggle in South Africa and our struggle as blacks in America, our host strongly suggested that we should pay a visit to Mr. Kwame Nkrumah, the former president of Ghana, who had fled to live in Guinea. Although I was flattered by the invitation, and would have loved to meet and talk with President Nkrumah, I was exhausted from traveling and wanted to get back home, and we still had our trip to Nairobi, Kenya ahead of us. After our goodbyes to our wonderful hosts and the others we met in Tanzania, we boarded the plane for Kenya.

While in Kenya we enjoyed sightseeing around Nairobi and visited several artisans whom we watched making statues and other works that they would sell. We were told by some of the Kenyans we met that there were a number of black Americans living in Nairobi. LaVerne and I found that to be very interesting, but our short stay in Kenya did not allow enough time to pursue that interest. However, we did happen to meet one black American who was visiting in Zambia. We talked with him for awhile and enjoyed meeting and talking with one other black American, which my brain realized that we had not seen a black American, other than the four Peace Corps volunteers, in almost a year. My brain recognized the absence.

CHAPTER NINE

From Africa to Business and Academia

Our stay in Kenya and in Africa came to an end—we had a marvelous experience. Our lives were so enriched and broadened. I felt that I was returning to America with a broader experience and an increased determination to do whatever I could to address the problem of racism in America. Our long flight to Washington DC was an endurance test for me of the worst kind, but we made it safely, retrieved our luggage, and took a taxi to LaVerne's sister's house, where we would be staying while I was being debriefed from the Peace Corps.

My debriefing was rather brief, I thought. I met once with the national director and we talked for a short while about things that seemed to be of no real consequence. I was leaving the Peace Corps prematurely and I was never asked for the reasons why I decided to leave early. I really never knew what he or other Peace Corps officials felt about my leaving before my four-year term of duty was completed. Perhaps it was not an important item to them, or maybe they just didn't want to hear what I had to say.

Either way, it was time for me to get on with my life, and time for LaVerne and me to get back home to San Diego. We were not able to take my sons with us to Africa because they were living with their mother, so I was more than anxious to get back to San Diego to be with them. LaVerne loved San Diego and she was anxious to get back as well.

However, when I left the Peace Corps I was unable to find a teaching position in San Diego. So instead, I accepted an invitation from my friend, Floyd McKissick, who was the past national director of CORE and an attorney. Floyd and I served on CORE's National Action Council and became good friends. Floyd became the national director of CORE replacing Jim Farmer who was the founder and the national director. I saw Floyd in an elevator in Washington, DC and he asked me if I would be interested in joining with him to form a company in New York to provide startup and seed capital to minority-owned businesses. Since I was unable to find a position in San Diego, I told Floyd I was interested and I would discuss it with LaVerne. LaVerne reluctantly supported my accepting Floyd's offer on the condition that I would continue to explore employment opportunities in San Diego.

Floyd had already formed his company and named it Floyd McKissick Enterprises. He had a commitment from Chase Manhattan Bank to provide seed capital to get his company started and he secured an office in Harlem. Floyd hired me as his Executive Vice President. I was very excited about being in the business to provide capital for minority businesses. Economic development in minority communities has been a long-time interest of mine.

LaVerne and I rented an apartment in Harlem and she accepted a position with IBM Corporation in New York. Floyd had plenty contacts, so he pursued raising capital as we looked for potential clients. One of Floyd's ideas was to develop a black city that would be named Soul City. I loved the idea although I didn't have a clue as to how that could be accomplished. We pursued the Soul City idea with Floyd's eyes focused on some land in North Carolina. Floyd contacted the company that was developing a new city that would be named Columbia, to be located between Baltimore, Maryland and Washington DC. Floyd arranged for us to visit with the Columbia developers so we flew to the site to get information on how they were developing this new city.

We spent the day with the developer and his team. At the end of the day, the developer suggested to Floyd that I stay at Columbia and learn from them how a city is developed. I was not interested in that idea at all and apparently neither was Floyd. I worked for McKissick Enterprises for eight months and felt that I wanted a position that would allow me an opportunity to be in the business world where I could learn how businesses operate.

Later, I met the Dean of the business school at Columbia University while working at McKissick's, and he offered to send my resume to several companies in New York. Marine Midland Bank of New York was one of those companies. Marine Midland called me to come in for an interview. I went in, was interviewed and hired. I was placed in the bank's management training program, which I later learned I was the first Negro to go through their management program. Banking was a new experience for me, and one that I learned to like. I had been a schoolteacher, a civil rights leader, and a Peace Corps administrator. I was now becoming a banker, a completely new experience.

My Experience at Marine Midland Bank, New York

At Marine Midland I was learning a lot about banking and the business world. It was very fortunate for me to have a person at the head of the bank that took an interest in me and wanted me to become a successful banker. His name was Charlie Mansfield. I don't know how he knew about me, but since I was the first Negro hired into their management training program, I guess that explains it. It's interesting to note that I didn't see myself as a "Negro" looking for a job. I was just looking for a job because I needed a job.

At any rate, Charlie Mansfield was a great help to me and I am thankful and very appreciative of the support he gave me. I feel sure that I would not have been hired by Marine Midland Bank without Charlie Mansfield's approval. When I completed the employment application at Marine Midland, I did not indicate that I had ever been arrested. The reason I didn't was because it was my understanding from one of the judges who sentenced me, that after a period of time, and after my two-year probation was over, my jail record would be expunged, and there would not be a record of my serving time in jail.

After I had been hired at Marine Midland I was called into the personnel office and asked why I did not answer yes to the question "were you ever arrested?" I answered the question and I never heard any more about it. I went through the management training program enjoying and learning how to be a banker.

I was enjoying my time at the bank and received several promotions, but I needed to get back to San Diego to be with my two sons who needed me, and I felt guilty and unhappy about not being with them. So, I contacted my friends in San Diego when I learned that the San Diego Urban League was looking for a president. I talked with a friend who was on the Urban League Board of Directors and expressed my interest in applying for the position, but I never heard from him or anyone in the Urban League. Months passed and upon completion of the management training program I was promoted to the position of Assistant Commercial Banking Officer, which at that time was a big deal to become a baking officer at a large Wall Street bank. I then learned that a group in San Diego was starting a "black bank." I called my friend in San Diego to find out who was organizing the bank. I happened to know several of the organizers, so I contacted one of them and explained that I was employed as a commercial loan officer at Marine Midland Bank in New York and that I was very interested in applying for a position in their bank and returning to San Diego. I never heard from him or anyone else of the organizing group.

By now, I had been with Marine Midland Bank for over two years and had completed the Masters degree in business administration at Fordham University. One evening I received a telephone call from a friend in San Diego, Vernon Sukumu, who was a student at San Diego State University at the time. Vernon said that San Diego State was interested in hiring a person to be the assistant to the president and asked if I would be interested in applying. This was 1971 and San Diego State was having its problems with student unrest, as colleges were around the country. San Diego State needed someone in the university administration to be the assistant to the president who could organize the black studies program and supervise the Employment Opportunity Program for minority students.

I sent my resume to Vernon and he forwarded it to the administration at San Diego State and recommended that they should offer the position to me. After speaking by phone with the university's representative, I submitted an application and was hired. I will forever be thankful and indebted to Vernon Sukumu for notifying me about the position and submitting my name. We were finally going home to San Diego, and now it was time for LaVerne and me to say our goodbyes.

I said goodbyes to my friends at the bank and to our friends we made while living in New York. I said goodbye to Harlem where I enjoyed and loved living. LaVerne said goodbyes to her friends at IBM Corporation. We packed our things and headed home. LaVerne received a transfer to the IBM office in San Diego, so we both were as happy as we could be.

San Diego State University

It was now September 1971 and I was now beginning another new career, college administration. My title was Assistant to the Vice President for Academic Affairs and the Assistant to the Vice President for Administration. When I arrived to begin my employment, the vice president for academic affairs had been appointed to the position of Interim President. So, I became assistant to the president and assistant to the vice president. My 33 years at San Diego State University were very pleasant and productive. When I started in my position, I could not have asked for a better group of associates to work with: Dr. Don Walker, who was the interim president, Dr. Ned Joy, vice president for academic affairs, Dr. George Gross, and Dr. Adrian Kohanski. These were my immediate coworkers whom I worked with on a daily basis. It was a joy to work with them and become their friend. I was fortunate to start my career at San Diego State in such a welcoming environment. All four of these men were a number of years my senior, and all of them are now deceased. I miss them very much.

Developing a Black Studies Program

Two of my immediate tasks were to organize and develop a black studies program, which currently consisted of a few courses taught by a few black faculty members who were lecturers and not on the tenure track. The other task was to supervise the Economic Opportunity Program, which was created to provide assistance to minority students. Since I was such an enthusiast of the study of black history, I poured everything I had into developing a strong black studies program. With the full support of the president of the university and his staff, I was able to obtain faculty positions to hire full-time tenured faculty and staff positions to form a solid black studies program. I also added a component to the black studies program to provide counseling to black students. San Diego State was a predominantly white college with approximately one percent or less of the student population was black. I felt that a counseling program was needed to support black students at a predominantly white college. I named the black studies program the School of Afro-American Studies, and set my goal to accomplish the following: (a) develop a curriculum; (b) recruit and hire full-time tenure - track faculty; (c) develop a major and minor in Afro-American studies; (d) have courses in the School of Afro-American studies program that would fulfill the general education requirements of the university. All four goals were achieved during the two years I served as the director of the program.

Fulfilling the university's general education requirements was quite an accomplishment because in 1972 I don't believe there were any universities that were predominantly white that had a black studies program that contained courses that fulfilled the general education requirements of the university. The significance of this accomplishment is that it placed the Afro-American studies program on the same footing as the other departments of the University.

Remember, what most of us learned in America about the colors black and white, we know that black studies programs were perceived by most people as a "black" program to appease black students and prevent further student disruption. To develop a quality academic curriculum with a major and minor concentration, high-quality faculty with doctorate and having courses that fulfilled the university's general education requirements, nullified the image of Afro American Studies at San Diego State being just some black program. The fulfillment of the university's general education

Initial Program Cover for San Diego State University's Black Studies

YOUR GOAL — OUR GOAL
EXCELLENCE IN EDUCATION

The School of Afro-American Studies has set its goal--Excellence in Education. The school is designed to serve the particular needs of Black people in pursuing that goal.

We take the prerogative to distinguish Black education from the traditional education received by Black people from white controlled institutions. We accept the challenge to provide an educational experience that will be conducive to the psychological and intellectual growth of Black people.

The School embraces the goal of Excellence in Education with much enthusiasm and we urge you-the students-to join us as we work toward that goal.

Harold K. Brown
Director

requirement also made it more attractive to white students and to the black students who may have shied away from blackness. I was very thankful to my administrative associates and friends who supported my efforts in accomplishing what we did for the Afro-American studies program.

The Afro-American Studies curriculum was developed through the hard work of the Afro-American studies faculty, under my direction. We put in many hours, days, evenings, and weekends as the faculty members developed the course they taught, and prepared their courses to be submitted to the university for its approval. I felt it was a remarkable effort and a remarkable achievement.

I felt it was also quite an achievement to offer a counseling program to augment the Afro-American studies program. To accomplish this I asked a close friend of mine, psychologist Dr. Norman Chambers, who was one of the few black professionals who participated with us in CORE's demonstrations, if he would consider organizing a counseling program as a component of the School of Afro American Studies and join with us as a faculty member at SDSU. He said yes to my invitation.

There was one more thing that I wanted to accomplish with Afro-American studies. Norm Chambers and I came up with the idea of changing the name School of Afro-American Studies to the School of Ethnic Studies that would house a number of ethnic programs and would qualify to have a dean and other administrators. I was excited about that idea, but I was not able to get it accomplished. So, after completing two years as the director, I decided that the School of Afro American Studies was off to a good start and I could now turn over the director's position to someone else, and I could continue pursuing my career goal as a college administrator. I asked Dr. Francis Foster, who taught English Literature in the School of Afro-American Studies and who had been teaching English Literature as a course in black studies when I started my employment at the university. My goal was to become a president of some college or university one day. I thought I would be able to accomplish the three goals I had set for the Afro-American studies program in a year, but that was wishful thinking, so I stayed as the director for a second year.

In 1972, my second year with Afro-American studies, I was promoted to the position of Associate Dean for Planning. The University had hired a new president, Dr. Brage Golding, and I reported directly to him. I received a call from the president one day to come to his office. He asked me if I would be interested in a position to organize the computing/data processing operation for the campus. He explained that the university's computer operations needed to be organized and with my skills and interests in management and administration, he would like to have me as the director of Campus Information Systems. I told him I was interested but I would need to have the authority to make the changes I felt necessary to create and develop a data processing department. He assured me that I would have that authority. I told him I would be glad to accept the position.

I spent the next five years organizing and directing the data processing operation for the university and repairing a severely damaged relationship between the campus and the chancellor's office.

When I began my duties as the Director of Campus Information Systems, I inherited a hotbed of resistance. It became obvious that some of the staff persons were displeased with my being placed in charge of computer operations for the university and felt that the person who had been managing the operation should have been made the director. I received half-hearted support from the person who had been in charge of the operation, and from those who were loyal to him. I made a number of changes in the operations of data processing and upgraded the University's IBM computer to a more updated IBM model, which the university, for years was unable to accomplish. I also organized the people who were directors of data processing at the campuses of the California State University (CSU) system to form an organization to work with the Chancellor's office to coordinate data processing in the CSU system. I served as the organization's first president. Through my efforts, our campus and the chancellor's office developed a much better working relationship. But during my tenure as Director of Campus Information Systems, the resentment I felt coming from some staff members at our campus computer center never changed. However, I was fortunate to have a secretary who was not only a highly proficient person; she was very supportive and loyal to our office.

I suppose I could have concluded that the hostility I felt which came from members of my staff at the computer center was the color monster popping its head up again. However, that is not my conclusion. I believe that the problem was that I was appointed to the position of director, which they felt should have gone to their leader who had been managing the data processing staff. I'm sure the color of my skin did not help the situation. Actions caused by the color monster are sometimes hard to detect. But those of us who have lived with that monster all our lives, are very good at recognizing it when it appears.

I never heard of any complaint from the staff that I did not have a computer or data processing background, which I did not, or that I did not have the ability to manage the computer operations. Yet, one of the staff members went to the president of the University and complained that the computer system that I purchased to run on our computer would not work. The president assigned the complaint to a vice president who agreed with the staff person. Of course, the system ran very well on our computer. We had an IBM computer, which I purchased from IBM, and I had an IBM Systems Engineer at home, my wife, who was an IBM Computer Systems Engineer who installed large computer systems throughout San Diego. The color monster had a way of making people do strange things. I think this was an example of that. We see it with our brain that is filled with personal racial history. Besides, I am sure none of my staff had ever worked under a black manager and it probably was a shock to their nervous system.

After serving five years as the Director of Campus Information Systems, the College of Business Administration offered me a position as the college's Associate Dean for External Relations. I said my goodbyes to my colleagues and friends in the computer world, and began my duties in the College of Business. I was very excited about my new position because it connected me closely to San Diego's business community. I enjoyed developing the Office for External Relations and remained with the College of Business Administration for 26 years, until my retirement in 2004.

My Tenure in the College of Business Administration

My love for business has always been strong. I have always wanted to own a business since I was a kid. The closest I ever came to owning a business was my owning a wagon, buying a block of ice and an ice shaver, making a picture of Kool-Aid, and selling snow cones on the streets. My other experience as a kid business owner was making a shoeshine box, buying the brush, a shine rag and some shoe polish, and shining the shoes of my uncles and other visitors to our home. Ten cents a shine and five cents for a snow cone was big money for a little kid. The two and a half years that I was employed at Marine Midland bank in New York strengthened my desire to own a business. So when the College of Business Administration came knocking, I was overjoyed. The college was looking for a person to develop relationships with the communities outside of the campus and to raise funds for the college. I was approached by Dr. Ned Joy, the Vice president for Academic Affairs, my former administration colleague and friend, who asked me if I would be interested in the new position. I emphatically said yes. I was offered the position and became the Associate Dean for External relations.

It has been my belief since my senior year in college that business and economics should be a major part of the African American community's fight to become full participants as American citizens. So whenever and wherever I could get a listening ear, I would talk about the need for a program in business and economics that could be offered to people where enrollment in college is not necessary or needed.

It so happened during my tenure in the College of Business Administration that the National Accreditation team was coming to review the College of Business Administration for renewal of the colleges accreditation. It is my understanding that the accreditation team wanted to know what involvement the college had with its surrounding communities. I then received a call from the dean of the college who asked me to come by so we could talk about the community program that I had been talking to him about for years.

I told him that we should have a program that teaches how to use business and economic skills as tools for improving communities. He agreed and I was asked to develop such a program. I contacted Dr. Michael Swack, who was the Director of the Community Economic Development program at Southern New Hampshire University. Michael put me in touch with his associate and the two of them provided me with materials that helped me to develop a set of courses that dealt with the skills needed to apply to the development of communities.

I then recruited faculty members from our business college, along with a few from the city of San Diego, to teach the courses in the program. I also taught a course in the program, Introduction to Community Economic Development and I named the program Community Economic Development (CED). It was an eight-month program with classes on Saturdays. This was an exciting time for me. I was again directing the program that I felt was desperately needed by so many in underserved communities who wanted to help improve their communities. I have been fortunate in life to have had the privilege of directing the San Diego chapter of the Congress of Racial Equality, the university's Afro-American studies program, the Self Help Through Neighborhood Leadership program, the Black Economic Development Task Force, the Community Leaders Undoing Biases Program, and the university's Community Economic Development (CED) Program. Each of these programs was aimed at equipping the participants with the knowledge and skills to address the needs of the underserved communities.

The goal of the Community Economic Development Certificate Program (CED) was to carry out the mission of producing technically competent and community-minded economic development professionals, and to produce graduates committed to the principle that residents of neighborhoods and communities should play a major role in the development of their areas.

Community economic development is an innovative and practical approach to helping communities and neighborhoods prosper through the use of business, economic, and leadership skills. Community economic development is a systematic and planned intervention that is intended to promote economic self-reliance for communities and the residents.

The CED program was established in 1995, and offered courses in finance, accounting, marketing, community organizing, organizational management, small business development, sources of capital, real estate and land development, and legal structures. The program's courses were held on Saturdays throughout the academic year, and were taught by San Diego State University faculty and a few members from San Diego's business and civic communities.

In the year 2000, I recommended to the dean of the business college that we change the name of the CED program to the Center for Community Economic Development. My request was approved and our center's program then appeared in the university's catalog under the College of Business Administration. Most of the students who enrolled in the program were college graduates, some with degrees beyond the baccalaureate level, and they represented a variety of ethnic backgrounds.

At the time when I retired in 2004 the Center had graduated 222 students since the beginning of the program 1995. The ethnic breakdown of the students was 36% Caucasian, 30% African American, 17% Hispanic American, 9% Asian American, 4% African, 2% Multi-racial, and 2% other.

The Center for Community Economic Development enjoyed widespread support from San Diego's business, government, and civic communities. With the designing of the curriculum of activities for the Leadership Training Program in 1966 to include economics, to the development of the Black Economic Development Task Force, to the Center for Community Economic Development - these programs were well received by the community residents, the business and government communities and San Diego State University.

An example of the acceptance and realization of the value of these programs, I was chosen by the U.S. Small Business

Administration to receive the Minority Small Business Advocate of the Year Award for the United States. I was very proud to receive this award on behalf of those who helped to form and administer these programs.

The success of the CED Program at San Diego State University was recognized through the praise from various organizations and news articles. I was especially proud to have received in 2002, the Richard Preston Award from the International Economic Development Council. The Richard Preston Award honors an economic development practitioner who has demonstrated excellence in "continuing education". I was very pleased to have received this honor on behalf of San Diego University, my CED Advisory Committee and my very competent assistant director, Linda Guzzo.

The Community Economic Development Program became a certificate program and was very successful. Many of the students who graduated from the program gave the program very high marks, and the university received very good public relations for offering such a program to the San Diego community.

Headline and story in local newspaper

However, my attempt to have the CED program offered in the business college curriculum as a major and not as a certificate program was not successful. After seven years of directing and teaching in the CED program, I retired from the university. The CED program was discontinued two years after I retired. I don't know the reason, but my guess is that the funding for the program was not there because the university's funds were needed elsewhere and I was no longer there to raise the funds that supplemented the university's share.

Black Economic Development Task Force meeting

The Black Economic Development Task Force

I remained active in the San Diego community as a volunteer in various organizations, during my tenure as an administrator at San

Me speaking at Black Economic Summit

Me speaking at Black Economic Summit

Diego State University. In 1987, a black summit was held at Lincoln High School and I was asked to write a paper on black economic development in San Diego. I wrote the paper and submitted it to the chair of the summit. I chaired a workshop on black economic development at the summit, and out of that discussion came the idea of forming the Black Economic Development Task Force (BEDTF) organization. We organized the task force and I served as its chairman.

The task force was very active in the community. It introduced into the San Diego community the words "Black Economic Development." These three words used together in the 1980s were difficult for people's brain to accept and difficult for people to say, but the activities of the task force over time made it comfortable for people to say understand the phrase over time.

The task force held regular meetings to discuss and teach the concept of black economic development. It raised funds from the business community, the city of San Diego, and a private foundation. The task force held four economic summits during its ten years of existence. The summits brought together San Diego's black-owned businesses, creating the opportunity for these businesses to purchase tables to display and promote their goods and services. The summits provided workshops on various informative topics on black economic development, which attracted many attendees. Each summit presented a featured luncheon speaker.

The task force also provided free business counseling to black entrepreneurs. I feel that the Black Economic Development Task Force was a very successful program and I am very proud of its contribution to the San Diego community and particularly to San Diego's black community.

A great success of the BEDTF was its project to break down the barriers of racial discrimination at San Diego's International Airport. There had never been a minority-owned business located in the airport. BEDTF took on the challenge of breaking down the door of racial segregation to minority owned businesses.

I put together a group representing various ethnicities to force the airport to open its doors to businesses owned by people of color and women. We named our group Communities United for Economic Justice (CUEJ). I was the chairman and spokesperson for the group. CUEJ's members included the San Diego Urban League, Catfish Club, NAACP, Indian Human Resource Center, Union of Pan Asian Communities, Asian Business Association, Chicano Federation, Coalition of Hispanic Professionals, and the Women Business Community.

Tony Brown (2nd from left), former Congressman Jim Bates, and me at Black Economic Summit

These organizations joined together to fight for economic justice at the San Diego International Airport. After many meetings with the San Diego Port Commission, CUEJ was able to convince the Port Commission to not renew the contract with Host International, the company that controlled which businesses were accepted to operate at the airport, until minority-owned businesses were included in Host's contract. CUEJ's well-fought battle for the inclusion of minority-owned businesses at the airport was successful, and a major step forward for San Diego.

MEETING WITH EDITORIAL BOARD OF SAN DIEGO UNION TRIBUNE

Me speaking to San Diego Union Tribune Editorial Board

Me receiving U. S. Minority Small Business Advocate Award

CHAPTER TEN

Real Estate and Land Development

I have a love for economics, and a strong belief that economics can play a major role in our "black struggle." If utilized right, it can help us shed the legacy of slavery and Jim Crow, and forge our way to the front of this country that we contributed so heavily to build.

When I was employed as a commercial loan officer at a major bank in New York City, during which time I was earning a Master's Degree in business administration, I was even more convinced that we as black Americans should master and use the tools of business and collective economics to power our way further down the road toward our liberation.

At the time, I decided to put to use what I learned while working at the bank in New York City. While at the bank, I learned about a program that provides capital to minority-owned business. This program by the federal government—called MESBIC, Minority Enterprise Small Business Investment Company—provided up to four dollars for every dollar that the MESBIC would raise. I felt that this would be a great tool to be used by black entrepreneurs.

I raised some seed money to get a business plan written and received a commitment from a local philanthropist for the $500,000 required by the federal government to license a MESBIC. I also had a commitment from a bank to participate if I could raise the remainder of the $1 million. Before I could raise the remaining amount however, a couple of Caucasian men decided that they would start a bank in Southeastern San Diego, a predominantly black populated section of San Diego at the time.

These two fellows were able to receive the blessing of the organization known as the Catfish Club, a predominantly black organization in Southeastern San Diego. Although the bank group was aware of my efforts to form a MESBIC, they didn't contact me until the local philanthropist's executive assistant informed them that they should. They reached out and we had lunch, but they were not interested in changing or modifying their plans.

After two years of work in trying to form a MESBIC for San Diego, I decided to abandon the idea. I was deeply disappointed that the black community did not support the formation of the MESBIC which could have been a great boost to the San Diego minority community. This was a great loss.

After my retirement from the university I decided to devote more time to my interest in real estate and land development. Over the years, I have invested in real estate. I started by buying a house to rent out and later bought duplexes to rent out. My full time involvement in real estate investing started when I was approached by a man who had bid on a project to build homes on a parcel of land located in a neighborhood in Southeastern San Diego. Most of the residents in that neighborhood where I previously lived were black. This man, prompted by the woman heading the Southeastern Economic Development Agency, Carolyn Smith, who had suggested that he might want to invite a minority partner, asked if I would be interested in being a partner on this project. I said yes and I invited my close friend, Joe Outlaw, to participate with me. This man, along with Joe and me, then formed a partnership to bid on the project.

Me with business partners Joe Outlaw and Michael Grant

The project was awarded to us and we built 52 luxury homes on that parcel of land. We each took an equity share, hired a general contractor/developer, Michael Grant, owner of the Grant Companies, who also became an equity partner, and we proceeded to secured bank financing. I took money from my retirement fund and I invested it into the project. The project was extremely successful. When the project ended in 1995, Joe and I, along with our general contractor/builder, Michael Grant, formed a Limited Liability Company (LLC), named BTW Development, Inc. to continue doing real estate projects. We have been doing real estate projects together ever since. The projects increased in size and included single homes, shopping centers, and storage facilities. Michael Grant's company

Michael Grant, me, and Joe Outlaw reviewing construction plans for model homes

is currently building a resort housing community for seniors, a 500-residence development of which my wife and our son Steve and daughter-in-law, Marisa, are investors.

At this point in my life, with having had great success in investing in real estate, I am told by some of my friends that I should now take it easy and ride off into the sunset with my wife and enjoy myself. Well, my wife and I are enjoying ourselves without riding off into the sunset. We continue to be involved in our respective interests. My wife is an active member of her sorority, Alpha Kappa Alpha, and I am an active member of my fraternities, Kappa Alpha Psi, and Sigma Pi Phi. She and I are speakers at events when asked. I also act as an advisor and mentor to younger men who are providing leadership in their communities.

Building Community Wealth

My goal now is an attempt to tackle one more idea. I would like to do what I can to promote the idea of wealth building in the black community. I would like to see the focus be on the words "Build Wealth!" the same way we focused on the words "Freedom Now" in the civil rights movement. If that were to happen, I would then be ready to ride off into the sunset. Blacks, as a group have not focused enough on building personal and collective wealth. I know some have written about it, even produced videos to discuss the importance of building wealth, but we still as a group have not focused on using the American economy to produce the wealth that can be used to address some of the problems facing us as black people.

Obviously, with more wealth comes more capacity that can be directed toward education for our youth, capital for business investment, and the development of a stronger voice politically. I'm certainly not the first person to put forward this idea. I know there have been those who are much more capable than I, who have advanced this idea. Nevertheless, I can't stop wondering why this idea has not been adopted by the black community, especially by middle and upper income blacks. I'm not unaware of the enormity of such a challenge, but challenge is nothing new to the black community. It just seems to me that this is something we could do—something we need to do. With wealth building we don't have to picket or sit in, or march anywhere, or go to jail. All we have to do is think wealth building and act on it.

Economic power called key to civil rights that last

Headline of article in San Diego Union written by Graciela Sevilla, October 27, 1991.

I guess I will never get over being a civil rights and community activist and being told that things could not be done. We just went out and did them. I wish the same thing would happen with the idea of wealth building. I think most non African Americans still think of black America as being mostly poor and powerless, having very little political or economic clout. Whether this is true or not, it would serve us well to create the perception of a group of people that has wealth and significant political influence.

The idea I am presenting here regarding wealth building is certainly not a new idea among African Americans, as I have mentioned earlier. Black Americans have formed banks and insurance, real estate, and other companies for many years. Many years ago blacks in places like Atlanta, GA; Durham, NC; Tulsa, OK; and a number of other cities built very successful black business communities. In 1921, Tulsa, OK had such a thriving black business community called Black Wall Street, which was reported to have been burned down to the ground by jealous whites.

In San Diego, in 1963, an airlines skycap named Henry Hill formed an investment club, Timely Investment Club (Timely). Henry was a friend of mine. He was a terrific role model for me and others who were interested in saving and investing and building wealth for ourselves and our families.

I became a member of the club and worked closely with Henry, and I was quite close to the club's operations. I was still serving as the chairman of San Diego CORE when I joined Timely, but I was an enthusiastic and dedicated member of Timely. I brought in many members and the membership grew to over 500, and all the members were black except for a few. Each member purchased units of ownership at a minimum of $25 each month. This may not sound like much today but in the 1960s, it was a considerable amount for many to pay each month. It didn't take long for some of the members to increase their monthly investment beyond the $25 minimum. When I accepted the position as Deputy Director of the U.S. Peace Corps, and while my wife and I lived in Lesotho, Africa, we continued to send a check each month to Timely. In 1967, when we left San Diego for Lesotho, the members had invested over one million dollars into Timely Investment Club.

I continued to be an investor in Timely until it had the misfortune in the 1970s during the country's economic recession, of facing a membership that became fearful of losing their investment. So, there was a "run on the bank." The members wanted their money back. When Henry Hill tried to convince them that their money was safe and to leave their money there, things got worse. I tried to convince Henry to let me write a letter for his signature, and send it to the membership explaining that their money was safe, but he chose not to do it. The word spread throughout the membership that the members could not get their money and a lawsuit was filed against Timely. I never knew the details of the lawsuit, but Timely went out of business and LaVerne and I, and I suspect others, lost the money we had invested in Timely.

This may sound like a tragic story, but I would argue that it is not a tragic story, nor is it an ending. Yes, it is terrible that we members lost our money and Timely had to discontinue operating. But, Timely was successful in bringing together a large number of African Americans to form what must have been the largest investment club in America in terms of the number of members. It was quite an accomplishment that Timely could bring together more than 500 African Americans to pool their money by regularly saving an amount each month to invest. Timely introduced into San Diego's black community in the 1960s and 1970s, the concept of building wealth, at a time when the concept of economic development and wealth building had not been introduced into our black San Diego community.

The phrase "black economic development" was not used or understood by many in the black San Diego community. Further, Timely made a great contribution by introducing young men like me and young women to the idea of collectively building a vehicle to promote wealth in the black community. Henry Hill served as an inspiration to us younger blacks who could continue to work toward building wealth in the black community.

No, Timely was not a tragic story. It was a great idea and a great effort that did not reach its potential. The important thing to remember is that Henry Hill and the rest of us tried. Black people have always had to try - over and over again as our history shows us. We have come this far by trying, failing, and trying again.

I had a friend, who was also a member of Timely, say to me that he would never, ever invest with black people again. I was hurt by those words but I did not respond to them. I could only think that here is that color monster again. Only this time the color monster had affected my friend's brain, who was black, to the extent that he felt Timely failed because it was composed of black people. My friend was an intelligent, well-educated man who was well aware that many ideas and organizations started by whites did not accomplish what they set out to do. The same is true for any group of people regardless of the color of their skin. I'm sure other blacks felt the same about Timely as my friend did. My friend knew that, but the color monster is very strong and persistent. It can make you ignore all the education you have, and damage your ability to think logically.

I guess some of you who are reading this book are saying, okay, what are YOU going to do? Well, I have been thinking and talking about this for many years. At my age, with much less physical and mental energy than I had when I was younger, when I led San Diego CORE and other community organizations, I am still going to continue to try. I will attempt to form a capital formation group in San Diego that will have capital available to invest in projects that the group selects. This will be an attempt to demonstrate that we can work together to collectively invest our capital into profit making ventures and use some of the profits for scholarships for students who need financial assistance. When that group is successful, hopefully it will inspire others to join our group, or form a group of their own. The other thing I will attempt to do is create an organization to promote the concept of wealth building. This organization will present a series of short discussions on topics such as capitalism, free market, circulation of money, investing, and other topics related to building wealth. This program will be similar to the economic development program I developed for the business college at San Diego State University when I was the Associate Dean for External Relations.

A Case for Building Wealth: More Than One Trillion Reasons

What does it take to create wealth in the African American community that could be used to continue to uplift that community? The answer is simple: it takes capital to build wealth, and the will to do it. Collective wealth can be used for education, business development, job creation, health assistance, and political involvement. Some of our fraternal and civic organizations are doing a great job of helping in the area of education, but they could do so much more if they had more money to support their efforts. Much of the black organizations' income comes from outside the black community in the form of donations from businesses and philanthropic grants, with some coming from the members. The effort it takes for the members to receive these donations must be repeated annually, taking lots of energy from the members, and also money out of their pockets each year that could be used to support the other work they do. If the federal government classified community organizations based on income and net worth, like they do with households and businesses, most of the community organizations would be classified as being in poverty.

I find it interesting that the black population in the United States has annual spending power of more than one trillion dollars, and many of our youngsters can't find the money to go to college, or that many black-owned businesses are in dire need of loans and capital, and black colleges and universities are in need of financial support. More money needs to be available from blacks to spend on the issues facing the black community like high unemployment, high crime, low school graduation rates, health, poor housing, and of course lack of political representation.

One reason that more money is not available in the black community is because we spend most all, approximately ninety-five percent, of our trillion—plus dollars annually on things that have nothing to do with the issues I mentioned above, or we spend most all of that trillion—plus dollars purchasing goods and services from others who do not contribute to helping the black community progress. We as a black community are great consumers, but poor at saving and investing. How much stronger we would be as community if we came together to save and invest in profit producing ventures that would go toward addressing the problems mentioned above?

Tony Brown, who had a television program on KPBS years ago, talked about building wealth in the black community. He created a video that showed the spending patterns of black America. The video showed where and how much of annual black income was spent supporting businesses outside the black community and with non black owned enterprises. In his books, *Black Labor, White Wealth: The Search for Power and Economic Justice*; and *PowerNomics*, Claud Anderson speaks eloquently to the subject of black wealth. Of course, I'm not suggesting that all of the trillion-plus dollars black Americans spend each year should be spent with black-owned businesses and organizations. That is absurd and impossible. But much more should be spent creating more businesses that produce jobs. How can that be done? As I have said, it can be done through savings and investments. It can be done by saving and investing in for-profit ventures and using some of the profits to help address the problems mentioned above. Of course there is nothing new about what I just said. It's been practiced in America since America was born.

In case you don't recognize it, it's an important part of our country, called capitalism. Other ethnic groups save and collectively invest in for-profit ventures and then use their profits to enhance their lives. America is a relatively young country. It is still developing and building, rebuilding, inventing, and creating new technology. We, as African Americans need to be a part of America's growth as owners and investors and not primarily as consumers.

Can it be done? Of course it can. Black individuals have been joining together to invest their savings for years. My friend and I have been investing together very successfully for over 20 years. We have done very well in real estate development and we plan to continue. This is one small example. There are other small examples around the country, but what we need is large numbers of investors coming together to collectively invest in for-profit ventures. It amazes me that with all the middle and upper income black Americans that have been produced by education and the civil rights movement, we cannot join together to form the next civil rights movement "Blacks for Economic Progress" or whatever it might be called. Some of our great spokespersons of the recent past, such as Johnny Cochran, the well-known attorney for the O. J. Simpson case and others, called for reparations for black Americans. While much deserved, that issue seems to be all but dead. Using our own capital to further help underserved African Americans seems to me to be a logical and sure way to empower the African American community.

To form a large capital base we need to spend our money more wisely and save more. Maybe we need to spend less on luxury items, vacations, and conventions, and more on saving and investing. I realize the importance of being with large numbers of people from your organization under one roof, and the value of that synergy, but it is very costly. Then, we need to have a vehicle or vehicles where we can invest some of our savings. I recall reading in a magazine that showed a two-page diagram of all the investors' names who bought shares in Facebook's initial public offering. I looked for a black company or person on that list. Of course I found none that I recognized. The company's shares opened at 38 dollars per share in 2012 and five years later the shares are at 176 dollars per share. That is only one of many examples where opportunities to invest and build wealth occurred.

I know this example is on a large scale, but the point is that there are opportunities if we have the capital to invest, and are not afraid to invest it. Of course there are many opportunities for investment in real estate, which is the area where my wife and I have been successful. But there are other areas where we as blacks can collectively invest our capital.

Those of us who were activists and provided leadership in the civil rights movement, did not have the time or the knowledge and skills to think about economic development and wealth building. Remember, we were still fighting for job opportunities, the right to vote, and the right to live where we wanted. But now, those of us who have business degrees and degrees in economics should be the first to introduce the idea of wealth building in the African American community. While many of us have gained a large measure of individual success since the civil rights movement of the 1960s, we have failed to extend that movement into political and economic influence to address the problems affecting our black communities.

We have money, but it doesn't buy us any influence in America or solve the problems we have in our communities because collectively we have wealth, but individually we don't. I think we all know by now that the only way that black people will defeat the color monster is to defeat it ourselves, along with those who will join us. To depend on the government and others to do it for us is ignoring everything we have been told by black leaders and spokespersons of the past, from Frederick Douglass, Booker T. Washington, and W.E.B. Dubois, to Dr. Martin Luther King Jr. and Malcolm X., among many others.

CHAPTER ELEVEN

Destroying the Monster

The problem of the 20th century is the problem of the color line.
— Dr. W.E.B. Du Bois

These were the words of Dr. W.E.B. Du Bois, from his book *Souls of Black Folk*. Dr. Du Bois, who was born in 1868 and died in 1963, was a black American who was cherished and recognized as a genius. It would be impossible to intelligently argue that the color line is not also the problem of the 21st century.

As I have tried to point out in the writing of this book, color in America is a monster. It has caused more pain and destruction than any other issue in this country. Color is a disease created by America's founding fathers of this country and adopted by its citizens. I have tried to show you, the reader, how hundreds of millions of kids like the author of this book, could be affected by the use of color that confines those kids to substandard living conditions, which in turn could cause psychological damage, poor self-esteem, or the production of anger and aggressive or violent behavior.

In this book, little Hal Brown, along with his friends who he grew up with, navigated their way through the alleys and streets of their towns. Each town in America had its groups of Little Hal Browns growing up under those same horrid conditions. Little Hal grew up acquiring resentment along the way, only curbed by his success in sports and the caring and support of a few people with white skin. Little Hal Brown was eventually successful in holding off the color monster and acquired a number of successes, but many other Hal Browns did not. What a loss! I have often thought of the friends I grew up with, and the millions of other kids growing up in the 1940s and 1950s, who did not get a chance to receive higher education and, were restricted to no or low paying jobs. No, it was not easy fighting the color monster all your life. But it's a lot easier when you have a little money in your pocket.

How has the color monster hurt America? Besides losing all of the benefit of millions of black boys and girls who could have made significant contributions to America had they not been held back by color, America has spent billions of dollars over the years trying to keep the color monster alive and quieting those who protest against the actions caused by the color monster. Our country needs to eliminate all obstacles to kids who face the color monster every day of their lives.

What does the color monster look like? How would you recognize it? It hangs out in communities of color, which it had created many years ago with segregated housing. It has a real big smile on its face from the system it created to keep blacks at two or three times the unemployment rate of white people. You will recognize it when you read the list of Fortune magazine's top 500 companies and you don't see more than one black-owned company on the list, and that one company is fairly recent. You will recognize it when you look at the United States Supreme Court and you only see one black person, who happens to be a conservative who seems to be a friend of the color monster. The color monster reveals itself in the small amount of black net worth, low high school graduation rates, and high incarceration rates.

I believe we all know that the color monster was truly born in American slavery. The American system fed all of America the "Kool-Aid" that filled our brains to believe that slavery was okay because the slaves were black and really not full human beings. Laws and practices were put in place to enforce the acceptance of black people as inferior, that they need not be treated as humans. The color monster grew and became stronger through slavery, reconstruction, segregation, and discrimination. America grew stronger and the people who inherited white skin and enjoyed all the fruits and privileges of having white skin benefitted. We are now in the 21st century and we find that the color monster is alive and well. After the slave revolts, the emancipation and the civil rights movement, we as a country still find ourselves still suffering under the clutches of the color monster. The Ku Klux Klan still exists, along with other groups and individuals who want to take us backward and "Make America Great Again." But was an America that supported slavery, segregation, and discrimination ever great?

The civil rights movement, and all the work by many leading up to the civil rights movement, paid great dividends. Many gains were made to benefit people of color of which we are all proud. But, until we conquer the color monster, what we call racism will remain forever. So, what should we do to kill the color monster? The color monster has caused a lot of brain damage, so extreme care must be taken in the treatment to remove all the damage the color monster has caused.

First, white Americans who understand and appreciate what harm the color monster has caused in America must be willing to openly discuss the issue of race. America must become the country it professes to be and wants to be. To do this, white Americans should declare war on racism and the color monster. An example would be to join with blacks and other ethnic groups to form an organization and name it "Fighting Against Racism" (FAR). This organization would hold regular seminars and discussions on combating racism. The discussions would be directed toward helping to understand how racism and color have poisoned our society, and the steps we should take as a society to overcome this racial burden. The organization would speak out against racist groups and it would use the media to collectively and forcefully communicate its strong opposition to past, present, and future harmful acts directed at people of color. Now, I know what you are thinking, they are not going to do that! Maybe you are right. But if this isn't something they will do, then what will they do?

Secondly, blacks need to become very active members of an organization like FAR, working with white Americans and others to hold meaningful discussion on racism and race relations in America. Participants and membership in this organization should consist of churches, fraternities, sororities, community organizations, the National Association for the Advancement of Colored People (NAACP), and the Urban League, in addition to individuals. The organization should command widespread visibility of its strong stance against verbal or any other act believed to be committed because of racism. A similar organization was formed in San Diego by me and two white San Diego prominent business leaders. The organization was named Community Leaders Undoing Biases (CLUB). For ten years we held monthly lunch meetings at a local hotel and discussed various topics of race relations. The luncheon meetings attracted a number of participants from the San Diego business community and other parts of San Diego. The two business leaders who helped to form CLUB, Malin Burnham and Robert Payne, spent a considerable amount of their time with the organization, and they deserve, and have my and others' sincere thanks and appreciation. So, proposing the idea of FAR is not new in San Diego, only the name is different, as I pointed out above. I think we need a FAR organization today, or by any other name, to take on the challenge of really confronting racism.

In my opinion, since the assassinations of Dr. Martin Luther King Jr. and Malcolm X, black America has not had anyone who has been able to achieve that level of stature to articulate the problems of race in America. I don't think there is much likelihood that blacks will have another Martin Luther King Jr. or a Malcolm X anytime soon. Besides, we don't need one spokesperson: we need thousands, all spread out in cities and towns throughout the entire nation representing organizations like FAR.

Am I crazy or naive for thinking something like FAR could be created? I believe there is enough leadership in our communities to make it happen. We need to take the words of Nancy Reagan, the former First Lady who coined the phrase "just say no to drugs" and apply it to racism and say: "just say no to racism." FAR should be the battle cry of the rest of the 21st century.

Finally, let us not make the same mistakes many made before and during the 1960s civil rights movement. Let's become the militants of the 1960s that many disagreed with or for some reason shied away from supporting or participating. Let's stand up and speak loudly with one voice against racism. Let's make it uncomfortable for racism to exist.

The mistakes made in the past were for some to sit back and not confront racism. In the 1960s many viewed those who picketed, sat in, and went to jail protesting against the evils of racism as crazies, militants, troublemakers, and criminals. Now we need people like them, people like you, to declare war on racism. If we don't, America will suffer forever with this problem. Let's not take the chance of losing the millions of little Hal Browns who could be valuable contributors to our society. Let's go out and destroy this color monster.

FROM THE PROFESSOR

BY HAROLD K. BROWN

Racial Reconciliation

Don't you even think of not dealing with the problem as a serious disease

How are we going to address the race problem? It's probably the most difficult to solve among the many problems America faces. As a longtime San Diegan impressed with our biotechnology, I think it's a safe bet that cancer, AIDS and other major diseases will be eliminated long before the race problem.

The reasons for my prognosis are very simple. There is no resistance to eliminating diseases, an obvious benefit to people. And diseases are studied by groups of trained experts who apply the scientific method of research. The race issue is a social problem in which many people who have no training in the area of race will put themselves forth as experts.

Is the race issue important enough to even worry or think about? How does it affect us individually? It seems most of those who address the problem do so out of compassion. But that number is small. For most people there needs to be a crisis of some sort, a riot or mass protest or a blatant racial murder, before they will get involved.

Well, the race problem is a disease, a social disease. America contracted this disease when the slave ships carrying Africans from different parts of Africa arrived in Jamestown, Va., in 1619. When slavery was abolished in 1865 it was replaced with a system of white privilege and black suppression. The disease has plagued America for almost 400 years and its casualties have been the millions of people who were killed, died from overwork, died from a lack of medical care, or had their intellect and physical capabilities severely suppressed.

The disease began to receive some treatment and lots of attention during and after the 1960s civil rights protests and mass demonstrations. Those who participated, committed and sacrificed back then still deserve our gratitude. However, many feel the attention in the '60s was short-lived. and that things are getting worse. Race-hate incidents appear to be on the rise again and the division between white and black perceptions seems to be widening. Subtle and not-so subtle forms of racism still permeate our society.

So what can we do to help eliminate this disease? The following steps are recommended:

1. Get a "flu" shot to make sure you don't catch the disease, or visit a "doctor," someone knowledgeable on race problems, to see if you already have the disease. I'm pretty sure most of us already carry the malady and don't know it. The way to get a flu-type shot is to involve yourself in the discussion of the race problem in America. Learn about how it got started, what the problems are, how people feel about it and how you feel about it. Become knowledgeable so that you will recognize the symptoms of the disease when you and others display them.

2. Participate with a group that meets regularly for the purpose of discussing the race issue. Take some "courage and listening pills" before

each group meeting. They will help you to be a good listener and will give you the courage to say what you feel or to ask what you really want.

(Malin Burnham, Bob Payne and I co-founded Community Leaders Undoing Biases, CLUB, which meets for lunch the first Monday of each month at the Mission Valley Hilton. Join us, but please call for reservations first at (619) 594-6437. Ask around for other venues.)

3. Cultivate a friend who has a different skin color and cultural ethnicity from yours. Go to lunch or dinner with that person or couple or share a coffee break. Again, be sure to take your "courage and listening pills" and be up front about wanting to better understand the race problem.

4. Free yourself from guilt. Accept the reality of the history of America and its slave system and its treatment of its black citizens. Feeling guilty will not help. Understanding it, and taking steps to address the issues caused by that history, is the way to solve the race problem. No one can change the past but we can influence the future. If anyone feels guilty, it should be because he or she is doing nothing to contribute to the solution.

5. Be forgiving. This might be extremely difficult for many African Americans. But, if we are ever going to eliminate the disease, African Americans must find a way to overcome the feelings of resentment and bitterness and convert that energy to finding solutions. Forgiveness is part of the process of healing so that creative energy can be applied toward creative solutions.

So, African Americans had better take some 'forgiveness pills" before they start each day. One is prescribed in the morning before starting daily activities and one at bedtime to sleep better. These pills, like the "courage and listening pills," should be taken in consultation with a "doctor" so you will know when you can reduce the dosage or get off them completely.

Racial reconciliation will not happen until the bad memories of the past are overshadowed and blurred by the positive incidents of the present and the potential of the future.

What is the role of white citizens if African Americans are to be forgiving?

African Americans must see whites involved in the reconciliation process. They must see them

trying to educate themselves about the impact that race issues have had on their lives. They must see them making an attempt to grasp the subtle as well as the obvious racial put-downs. There must be a demonstration of willingness to join with blacks in support of those things that blacks consider to be important in their pursuit of the opportunities to participate fully in American society.

Involvement by whites and forgiveness by blacks will start a new era in America, "Racial Reconciliation."

6. Read black publications. This can be quite helpful in understanding the concerns of the African American population. It can be educational and entertaining. It will be quite helpful in your group discussions and with your friends at lunch or dinner and your associates at a coffee break.

There are a number of excellent magazines and many books written about the black experience, past and present. Join a book club that assigns books 10 read that are written by black authors or other authors who write on the topic of race in America.

7. Develop the habit of practicing race reconciliation on a daily basis. Practice it at home, at work or at play. Expect from your family, friends and colleagues an understanding of the race issue in America and an appreciation for its impact on citizens of color. Practice encouraging racial diversity at your workplace and find a way to address racial prejudices and myths.

The 20th century left us with a load of messy unfinished business. We did not apply ourselves sufficiently to the task of straightening out the race problem. We must do significantly better in the 21st. Everyone needs to work on the problem consistently until race in America becomes as insignificant as being right- or left-handed.

There is no better time to get started than February. The first African American History Month of the 2000s. My goal for 2000 is to make racial reconciliation and the elimination of the racial disease my top volunteer priority. I hope you will join me.

Harold K. Brown, who is semi-retired as an associate dean of SDSU's College of Business Administration, remains the director of its Center for Community Economic Development.

EPILOGUE

Today my life is full of love, understanding, and forgiveness, but I still can't help but think of all the little black kids of America who grew up under the same or similar or worse circumstances as I. What would they have accomplished if America had not forced them to live under such horrid conditions, to prevent them from rising above the lowest levels of existence? Many of those millions of black kids could have accomplished much more in life had they had the opportunities that their white counterparts had.

I can't help but look over my life and the lives of the boys and girls who I grew up with and the lives of my little nieces, nephews, and cousins. Many, like me, had parents who did not go beyond the eighth grade in school and lived in households of low income, and lived in a community that treated them as inferior human beings. How was a kid supposed to overcome those conditions and be competitive with whites who did not have to overcome such conditions?

Then I look at my life. I became a school teacher with a baccalaureate degree, which I would not have had if it had not been for my athletic skills which earned me a scholarship. I would not have had the opportunity to go to college and have a start in life toward becoming a school teacher, earning a master's degree, enrolling in a doctorate degree program and then receiving the highest honor a

Me, honored by The California Legislative Black Caucus

university can bestow upon an individual—an Honorary Doctorate Degree of Humane Letters from San Diego State University.

But what about my friends I grew up with? What were their chances of getting to college and earning a good start in life? I submit that they had very little chance. With the support and encouragement of my family, friends, and some very caring teachers, I became what

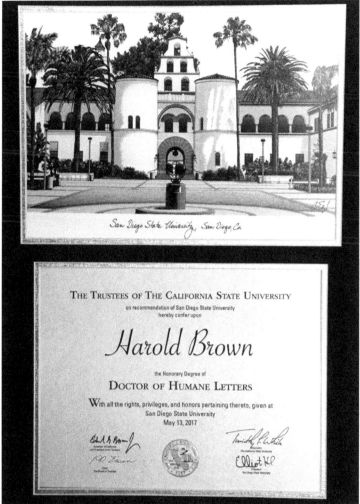

San Diego State University and a picture of my honorary Doctorate Degree

I believe to be a productive citizen. I was not one of the top students who qualified for an academic scholarship, so an athletic scholarship was my only hope. Thank God I had the athletic talent to merit a scholarship to college. But it has always been painful to realize that my friends who I grew up with, my extended family, did not have the same opportunity as I did.

I am thankful that since the time I graduated from high school, things have changed. There are many more black kids today who have a much better chance of going to college or a place of learning beyond high school. But there are still far too many who will not get that opportunity. So, what is the answer, or answers? How do we get those kids who want to go to college into college? The answers are so obvious that everyone knows what they are. America knows how to compensate for the conditions caused by slavery and Jim Crow, but America seems to be too busy with other things to address this problem. We as a nation have made considerable progress toward creating opportunities for the under-privileged, thanks to those organizations and individuals who led the way. But there is so much more to be done. It is up to you and me.

REFERENCES

BlackPast. "A Brief History of the San Diego NAACP, 1917-2007." *BlackPast*, 11 Dec. 2007, blackpast.org/african-american-history/brief-history-san-diego-naacp-1917-2007/.

Fikes, Robert, Jr. *The Struggle for Equality in America's Finest City: A History of the San Diego NAACP*, NAACP, 2012.

Mead, Margaret. Speech given when she received the Planetary Citizen of the Year Award, 1978.

The Fair Housing Center of Greater Boston. "1920s–1948: Racially Restrictive Covenants." *Historical Shift from Explicit to Implicit Policies Affecting Housing Segregation in Eastern Massachusetts*, n.d., bostonfairhousing.org/timeline/1920s1948-Restrictive-Covenants.html.

Davis, Mike, et al. *Under The Perfect Sun: The San Diego Tourists Never See*. New Press, 2005.

CPSIA information can be obtained
at www.ICGtesting.com
Printed in the USA
LVHW070536090819
627043LV00004B/50/P